*Fresh Lessons
from Former Leaders*

Books in the Stephen F. Olford Biblical Preaching Library

Fresh Lessons from Former Leaders

David, Elisha, Samson, Caleb, and Isaiah

Stephen F. Olford

BAKER BOOK HOUSE
Grand Rapids, Michigan 49516

Contents

Part 3 Meet These Men

Introduction

The Bible is full of people! Character studies, therefore, are a *must*! Read their stories over and over again. Research the meaning of their names, their historical backgrounds—and especially God's purpose in bringing them on stage. Then relate the supra-cultural principles and lessons they teach to your congregation. Nothing lives again like a Bible character preached in the power of the Spirit! Our Lord used character studies, as did the apostles.

In this fourth volume of the Stephen Olford Biblical Preaching Library we have a three-part series featuring the lives of David—"God's Man"; Elisha and his "Spiritual Secrets"; and finally, three characters—Samson, Caleb, and Isaiah—under the title "Meet These Men." You will enjoy preaching through these expository outlines. As you stylize these outlines to your own personality and pattern of preaching, remember what homiletical structure is all about. In the words of Ilion T. Jones: "The outlines should have *unity*, each point being a sub-thesis of the main thesis; it should have *order*, the points being coordinate; it should have *preparation*, all points being of parallel construction; it should have *climax*, the points being arranged in ascending order. The wording should not be odd, smart, or clever, but rather fresh, striking, and intriguing, without being sensational."[1]

I have had scores of testimonies from men of learning as well as beginners who have found spiritual and practical help for preaching from my sermon outlines. One such recipient of blessing writes: "I am a retired pilot who went into the ministry . . . from the cockpit to the pulpit. I use your resource materials often and they are a great help."

So I trust you, too, will profit from this volume. I exhort you, therefore, to "preach the word. . . . do the work of an evangelist, [and] make full proof of [your] ministry" (2 Tim. 4:2, 5 KJV). God richly bless you!

Stephen F. Olford

Part 1

God's Man: *David*

1

God's Man: *Introduction*

1 Kings 9:4; 11:4, 6, 38; 14:8; 15:5; Acts 13:22

"I have found David the son of Jesse, a man after my own heart, who will do all my will" (Acts 13:22).

Introduction

The life of David is one of the most illustrious, interesting, inspiring, and instructive of all the narratives in the Bible. His character is more fully portrayed than any other person in the Old Testament. Although David was guilty of adultery, murder, and many other of the deadly sins, yet he was said to be ". . . a man after [God's] own heart . . ." (Acts 13:22).

We shall understand this tribute to David's life if we remember that the person who lives closest to God's heart is not necessarily the one who lives most virtuously, but rather the one in whose life the moral struggle has been most faithfully maintained. There are people who may be more virtuous, because it is easier for them to live that way; but there is something heroic about the man who, all his days, has had to fight with moral infirmities and passion; who, though often conquered and crushed, has gotten up again with resolve in his heart and victory in his life.

David, the shepherd, singer, and sovereign, was such a man. He lived so close to God that he reflected aspects of the divine heart in the manner of his integrity, maturity, and fidelity. Solomon tells us that ". . . as [a man] thinks in his heart, so is he" (Prov. 23:7). Let us then consider the "heart" experience of David as an introduction to the more general studies that follow.

I. The Integrity of His Heart

". . . David walked, in integrity of heart and in uprightness, to do according to all that [was] commanded . . ." (1 Kings 9:4). The word "integrity" here denotes simplicity and is a key to the understanding of David's *personal life*, as revealed in the Psalms. Notice that he was a man who knew something of:

A. *Openness of Heart*

"Vindicate me, O LORD, for I have walked in my integrity. I have also trusted in the LORD; I shall not slip. Examine me, O LORD, and prove me: *Try my mind and my heart*" (Ps. 26:1–2). It is generally supposed that this appeal to heaven was written by David at the time when Ish-bosheth was assassinated by Bannah and Rechab, when David was protesting his innocence of complicity in that treacherous murder. With absolute integrity he calls upon God to search him thoroughly, to make a minute survey.

C. H. Spurgeon points out that there are three types of trial that are suggesting in the original; i.e., trial by touching, trial by smelling, and trial by fire. The psalmist was so clear of the charge laid against him that he submitted himself unconditionally to any form of examination which the Lord might see fit to employ. On another occasion David could pray, "Search me, O God, and know my heart; try me, and know my anxieties; and see if there is any wicked way in me, and lead me in the way everlasting" (Ps. 139:23–24). The dominant thought in this psalm is the omniscience and omnipresence of God. David knew that he could not hide from those eyes that burn as a flame of fire so he opens his heart to divine examination that he might be free of any wickedness that would lurk in the inner recesses of his being.

Illustration

Lafayette tells us that he was once shut up in a little room in a gloomy prison for a great while. In the door of his little cell was a very small hole cut. At that hole, a soldier was placed night and day to watch him. All he could see was the soldier's eye; but that eye was always there. Day and night, every moment when he looked up, he always saw that eye. Oh, he said, it was dreadful! There was no escape, no hiding; when he lay down and when he rose up, that eye was watching him.[1]

We can never flee God's presence (see Ps. 139:7–12). His eyes are constantly upon us—seeking, searching, probing, loving, guiding, correcting. With Hagar, Ishmael's mother, we can call the Lord, "You-Are-the-God-Who-Sees" (Gen. 16:13; see also Heb. 4:13). One day the eye of God will be on the sinner in judgment. How dreadful an occasion that will be!

B. Brokenness of Heart

"The sacrifices of God are a broken spirit, a broken and a contrite heart—These, O God, You will not despise" (Ps. 51:17). These are words that were wrung from David's heart after his fearful moral lapse. They occur in the prayer-psalm of penitence which he poured out before God after his serious sins of immorality, adultery, and murder.

There is a self-righteousness which would never descend to immorality of this kind; yet reflects a heart of stone almost incapable of penitence. God can do nothing with such hardness of heart. On the other hand, where there is brokenness and contrition there can be cleansing and forgiveness.

C. Truthfulness of Heart

When David asks, "LORD, who may abide in Your tabernacle? Who may dwell in Your holy hill?" he replies, "He who walks uprightly, and works righteousness, and speaks the truth in his heart" (Ps. 15:1–2). David wrote this psalm to depict the worthy worshiper. Though he lived hundreds of years before Christ, yet he was aware of the fact that ". . . those who worship [God] must worship in spirit and truth" (John 4:24). God cannot tolerate a lying heart in his presence. As the sweet singer of Israel puts it in another place, God desires ". . . truth in the inward parts . . ." (Ps. 51:6).

D. Holiness of Heart

Once again, David is thinking of God's holy presence, so he asks, ". . . who may stand in His holy place?" Back comes the answer, "He who has clean hands and a pure heart . . ." (Ps. 24:3–4). No wonder he cried out under the burden of his sin, "Create in me a clean heart, O God, and renew a steadfast spirit within me" (Ps. 51:10).

Are we characterized by such integrity? Is our heart open, broken, truthful, and clean? Can God say of our individual life, "I have found a man after Mine own heart, which shall fulfill all my will"?

Illustration

When the father of the great Emmanuel Kant was an old man he made a perilous journey through the forests of Poland to his native country of Silesia. On the way he encountered a band of robbers who demanded all his valuables, finally asking: "Have you given us all?" and only letting him go when he answered, "All." When safely out of their sight his hand touched something hard in the hem of his robe. It was his gold, sewn there for safety and quite forgotten by him in his fear and confusion. At once he hurried back to find the robbers, and having found them, he said meekly: "I have told you what was not true; it was unintentional. I was too terrified to think. Here, take the gold in my robes." Then to the old man's astonishment nobody offered to take his gold. Presently one went and brought back his purse. Another restored his book of prayers, while still another led his horse toward him and helped him to mount. They then unitedly entreated his blessing, and watched him slowly ride away. Goodness had triumphed over evil.[2]

II. The Maturity of His Heart

". . . when Solomon was old, . . . his heart was not loyal [or perfect] to the Lord his God, as was the heart of his father David" (1 Kings 11:4). The word *perfect* means "finished" or "whole," and suggests to us the maturity of David's *spiritual life*. To demonstrate this we turn, once again, to the Psalms, where we see something of the perfection of David's walk, worship, and witness.

A. *The Perfection of His Walk*

Addressing God, David says, "I will behave wisely in a perfect way. . . . I will walk within my house with a perfect heart" (Ps. 101:2). C. H. Spurgeon remarks that "this is just such a psalm as the man after God's own heart would compose when he was about to become king. It is David all over, straightforward, resolute, devout; there is no trace of policy or vacillations—the Lord has appointed him to be king, and he knows it, therefore, he purposes in all things to behave as becomes a monarch whom the Lord himself has chosen."[3]

When David says, ". . . I will walk within my house with a perfect heart" (Ps. 101:2) he realizes that piety must begin at home. The reality of a man is what he is in his heart and in his home. He cannot sing in the choir and yet sin in the office. He cannot be a saint in public and act like a devil at home.

Although David failed tragically at one point in his reign, yet there is every reason to believe that deep down in his heart he really wanted to walk wisely and perfectly before his God.

B. The Perfection of His Worship (Pss. 1–150).

This is where we are overwhelmed in attempting to select the best expressions of David's wholehearted worship. All his psalms are replete with expressions of adoration, thanksgiving, praise, and worship. For example: "I will praise You, O Lord, with my whole heart; I will tell of all Your marvelous works" (Ps. 9:1); and again: "I will praise You, O Lord my God, with all my heart, and I will glorify Your name forevermore" (Ps. 86:12); and still again: "Praise the Lord! I will praise the Lord with my whole heart, in the assembly of the upright and in the congregation" (Ps. 111:1).

Isaac Walton contends that David was said to be a man after God's own heart because he abounded more and more with thankfulness than any other person that is mentioned in holy Scripture. He points out that in the Psalms there is such a commixture of his confessing of sins and unworthiness, and such a thankfulness of God's pardon and mercies, as made him wholly acceptable to God.

One of the appalling evidences of immaturity in Christian experience today is the imperfection of worship. Gordon Dahl defines it this way: "Most middle-class Americans tend to worship their work, to work at their play, and to play at their worship. As a result, their meanings and values are distorted. Their relationships disintegrate faster than they can keep them in repair and their lifestyles resemble a cast of characters in search of a plot."[4] It is pathetic at times to listen to the attempts of some to offer their prayers and praises. In the light of David's devotional life, they have hardly begun. How tragic this is in a day when we have the full revelation of God as it is in Jesus Christ!

C. The Perfection of His Witness

Perhaps Psalm 40 seems to express David's witnessing heart best. Look at verses 1–3: "I waited patiently for the LORD; and He inclined to me, and heard my cry. He also brought me up out of a horrible pit, out of the miry clay, and set my feet upon a rock, and established my steps. He has put a new song in my mouth—Praise to our God; many will see it and fear, and will trust in the LORD." In view of such an experience of deliverance, direction, and devotion, David goes on to say in verse 10: "I have not hidden Your righteousness within my heart; I have declared Your faithfulness and Your salvation; I have not concealed Your lovingkindness and Your truth from the great congregation."

This is true maturity of experience. No one who has experienced God in such a deep way can be possessive of the gospel and hide it in their heart. It must be declared to all. It was the Lord Jesus who taught the same principle when he said, ". . . out of the abundance of the heart the mouth speaks" (Matt. 12:34).

Illustration

A man once laid a piece of chocolate candy on a table. Then, picking up an ant, he put it near the delicious bon-bon. He was surprised to see it take a single bite and then hurry off to inform the rest of the colony. Soon the little creature returned, followed by a long train of other ants who enjoyed the treat with him. Many Christians who have tasted that the Lord is good can learn a lesson from that little insect! Having found God's rich supply of grace, they ought to spread the glad tidings to others.[5]

III. The Fidelity of His Heart

". . . My servant David . . . kept My commandments and . . . followed Me with all his heart, to do only what was right in My eyes" (1 Kings 14:8). The phrase, "followed Me" indicates a "going on after," and suggests to us the fidelity of David in his *practical life*. This fidelity expresses itself first in David's allegiance, and then in his obedience to God.

A. His Allegiance to God

In a beautiful prayer recorded in Psalm 86:11, David says, "Teach me Your way, O LORD; I will walk in Your truth; unite my heart to fear Your name." A person with a divided heart can never be faithful to God; so David pleads for a united heart. The idea behind the word "unite" is that of union or conjunction, and suggests unity of purpose. As an adverb, the same word is rendered "together" and is used three times in Genesis 22, where ". . . the two of them [Abraham and Isaac] went together" (vv. 6, 8, 19). It is the opposite of being double-minded.

True allegiance, then, springs from a heart that is united to know God's way, to walk in his truth, and to fear his name. No wonder God could say of his servant: ". . . My servant David . . . kept My commandments and . . . followed Me with all his heart, to do only what was right in My eyes" (1 Kings 14:8).

With all his wisdom and privileges, Solomon did not follow the Lord in the same way. It is recorded of him that he ". . . did evil in the sight of the LORD, and did not fully follow the LORD, as did his father David" (1 Kings 11:6). In a day of faithlessness and irresponsibility on every hand, we need David's kind of allegiance to God.

B. His Obedience to God

In his psalm of testimony (Ps. 40), David could say, "I delight to do Your will, O my God, and Your law is within my heart" (v. 8). The literal translation of that last phrase is, "thy law is in the midst of my bowels." The Old Testament writers—and later the Greeks—located all feeling in the intestines. So the thought here then is that obedience to God was something of which he was always acutely aware.

The writer of the Book of Kings supports this in a comprehensive testimony to David's obedience. He says: ". . . David did what was right in the eyes of the LORD, and had not turned aside from anything that He commanded him all the days of his life, except in the matter of Uriah the Hittite" (1 Kings 15:5). Even in light of the grievous sin which David committed, the Spirit of God has recorded that the manner of his obedience was that he ". . . did what was right in the eyes of the LORD . . ." The measure of his obedience was that he ". . . had not turned aside from anything that He commanded him all the days of his life . . ." (1 Kings 15:5). Even when he did fall he got up again, sought cleansing and forgiveness, and pursued the same path of obedience.

Illustration

It is said of Henry of Bavaria that at one time, becoming weary of court life, he determined to enter a monastery. When he presented himself to Prior Richard, the faithful monk gave him the strict rules of the order. The king listened eagerly and enthusiastically expressed pleasure at the prospects of such complete consecration. Then the prior insisted that obedience, implicit and expressed, was the first requisite of sainthood. The monarch promised to follow his will in every detail. "Then go back to your throne and your duty in the station God assigned you," was the prior's word to him. The king took up his scepter again and from then until he died his people said of him, "King Henry has learned to govern by learning to obey."[6]

Conclusion

We have considered three characteristics of "the heart" experience of this sweet singer of Israel. In the integrity of his heart we have seen something of his personal life; in the maturity of his heart we have observed something of his spiritual life; and in the fidelity of his heart we have noted something of his practical life of allegiance and obedience. Little wonder that God could say, through the lips of the apostle Paul: ". . . I have found David the son of Jesse, a man after my own heart, who will do all my will" (Acts 13:22). Then the apostle continues: "From this man's seed, according to the promise, God raised up for Israel a Savior—Jesus" (Acts 13:23). A person whose integrity, maturity, and fidelity matches that of David is an individual through whose life God can reveal his Son Jesus, in all his saving grace, to a world of desperate need. As the chorus puts it, "What the world needs is Jesus, just a glimpse of him." God make us men and women through whom the beauty of Jesus can be seen.

How God Discovers His Man

1 Samuel 16

"The LORD does not see as man sees; for man looks at the outward appearance, but the LORD looks at the heart" (16:7).

Introduction

God is always looking for men and women whom he can "set apart" for some specific service. This is a solemn thought, when we remember that it can be said of each one of us, "There's a work for Jesus none but *you* can do." What a tragic thing it must be to be found unprofitable!

This, of course, raises the question as to how God discovers his man. The chapter before us gives the answer, for here is illustrated governing principles which determined God's choice of David—". . . a man after God's own heart . . ." (Acts 13:22). As we examine what God pleasurably discovered in this lad of fifteen years of age we notice that:

I. God Discovered Character in David

". . . the Spirit of the LORD came upon David from that
day forward . . ." (16:13). In *spirit* David was ". . . a man
after God's own heart . . ." (Acts 13:22); he had a spirit
which was alive unto God. In other words, before the day
of anointing, referred to in this chapter (16:13), David expe-
rientially knew the three essentials of spiritual character:

A. Fellowship in the Spirit

". . . the Spirit of the LORD came upon David from that
day forward . . ." (16:13). God was satisfied with David's
heart experience, and so witnessed to the fact by pouring out his Spirit upon him.

Notice in our reading that when Samuel interviewed
David's seven brothers God had to remind the prophet
that what mattered first was not appearance, but experience. ". . . the LORD said to Samuel, . . . man looks at
the outward appearance, but the LORD looks at the heart"
(16:7). In this respect God had found a man after his
own heart, who would fulfill all his will. There was that
"otherness" about David; in his presence one could
sense God.

There are other significant inferences given us in the
Scriptures which lead us to conclude that, though a lad,
David had a real experience of God in the fellowship of
the Spirit. Consider:

1. HIS DEVOTIONAL LIFE

Here we can draw on Psalm 23 where we read:
"The LORD is my shepherd; I shall not want. He makes
me to lie down in green pastures; He leads me beside
the still waters. He restores my soul; He leads me in
the paths of righteousness for His name's sake. Yea,
though I walk through the valley of the shadow of
death, I will fear no evil; for You are with me; Your
rod and Your staff, they comfort me" (vv. 1–4). It is

generally believed that this psalm was composed by David in the days when he shepherded his father's sheep. What depths of devotion and spirituality are reflected in these beautiful words!

2. His Vocational Life

When later he was brought before King Saul, David could testify of his experience in the Spirit, when he was up against danger and death. First Samuel 17:37 records his words: ". . . the LORD, who delivered me from the paw of the lion and from the paw of the bear . . . will deliver me from the hand of this Philistine . . ." Later, when facing Goliath, he could declare: ". . . I come to you in the name of the LORD of hosts, the God of the armies of Israel . . ." (1 Sam. 17:45). Fellowship in the Spirit was the basis and foundation of his character.

B. Faithfulness in the Spirit

The testimony of others concerning David was that he was ". . . a man . . . prudent [quick-witted] in speech . . ." (16:18). That expression is most enlightening and reveals something of the keenness, honesty, and faithfulness of this young man's service, whether by life or by lip. Whatever he said or did was, in a very real sense, to the Lord. In the realm of the spirit, he was ever conscious and aware of the fear of the Lord and of his stewardship of faithfulness. It was because he was so faithful in that which was least that, later, God made him faithful in that which was great.

C. Fearlessness in the Spirit

David is spoken of as ". . . a mighty man of valor . . ." (16:18). Even though a lad, he believed with all his heart that there is no danger in the path of duty. Later, when telling King Saul about his encounter with Goliath, he witnessed to his fearlessness in the Spirit. David could say: ". . . your servant used to keep his father's sheep, and when a lion or a bear came and took a lamb out of the flock, I went out after it and struck it, and delivered the lamb from its mouth; and when it arose against me, I caught it by its beard, and struck and killed it" (1 Sam. 17:34–35).

Solomon reminds us that "the fear of the LORD is the beginning of wisdom" (Prov. 9:10).

Illustration

Of all the memorials in Westminster Abbey there is not one that gives a nobler thought than that inscribed on the monument to Lord Lawrence—simply his name, with the date of his death, and these words: "He feared man so little, because he feared God so much."[1]

In the purpose of God, David was set apart because there was discovered in him the sterling character which springs from fellowship, faithfulness, and fearlessness in the Holy Spirit.

II. God Discovered Capability in David

The ". . . son of Jesse . . . who is skillful in playing . . ." (16:18). Here was a young man with a soul for heavenly music. There can be no capability without sensitivity. In other words, in *soul* he was a man after God's own heart. Within the humble and mundane sphere in which he had been placed David saw to it that he was one hundred percent capable. He was:

A. A Capable Shepherd

When Samuel inquired about him he was informed, ". . . he [was] keeping the sheep . . ." (16:11). Though he was the youngest of his brethren, he had showed himself so capable in the art of shepherding that his father was happy to leave all his sheep in his care. There is an impressive reference in chapter 17 which reveals how devoted to his job David was. Having been asked by his father to visit his brethren at the battle front we are told that ". . . David rose early in the morning [and] *left the sheep with a keeper . . .* " (1 Sam. 17:20). He saw to it that a suitable worker came to take over the responsibility of shepherding before he left for other service.

B. A Capable Singer

". . . skillful in playing" (16:18). He is also spoken of in another place as ". . . the sweet psalmist [singer] of Israel" (2 Sam. 23:1). He was a capable musician, composer, and singer. He believed that God's endowments and gifts should be developed and exercised to the best of his capabilities.

C. A Capable Soldier

". . . a mighty man of valor, a man of war . . ." (16:18). Moffatt renders these words as "a brave man, a soldier." He had proved himself an expert marksman with the sling, a fearless fighter with his shepherd's rod, and in all a capable soldier.

Such capability brought pleasure to the heart of God, not because of any intrinsic value in shepherding, singing, or soldiering, but because David was a man who believed and practiced "nothing but the best" for God. He strove for excellence both in character and capability. Truly, he was a man after God's own heart!

III. God Discovered Comeliness in David

". . . Now [David] was ruddy, with bright eyes, and good-looking. And the LORD said, 'Arise, anoint him; for this is

the one!'" (16:12). In *body* he was a man after God's own
heart. Far too little emphasis is placed upon the health of
the body, in our Christian teaching. We fail to remember
that when we are born again our bodies become the very
temples of the Holy Spirit. We forget that the fact of the
Incarnation places a sacred and high value on all believers'
bodies. This is why Paul tells us to ". . . glorify God in
[our bodies] . . ." (1 Cor. 6:20).

This view of our bodies casts no reflection on those
who, through no fault of their own, are called upon to suffer. Indeed, the suffering body can be the instrument of
even greater glory. Paul experienced this when he proved
that God's grace is sufficient for an afflicted body, since
divine strength is made perfect in human weakness. He
could say, ". . . most gladly I will rather boast in my infirmities, that the power of Christ may rest upon me" (2 Cor.
12:9). David would have never become such a man of
physical fitness and enduring strength, had he not cared
for the body which God had given him. The chapter before
us reveals that he was:

A. Physically Healthy

". . . Now he was *ruddy* . . ." (16:12). This word
denotes that he was healthy and strong. Unless a Christian is called upon, in some sovereign and mysterious
way, to suffer physically, there is no reason why he
shouldn't be one hundred percent healthy. Indeed, it
is his duty to God to see to it that he takes sufficient
exercise to keep his body ruddy and healthy. Paul's
instructions to Timothy (who was undoubtedly threatened by physical weakness) was ". . . bodily exercise
profits a little . . ." (1 Tim 4:8). Every believer should
diligently seek, by good diet, adequate sleep, and
proper recreation, to keep his body fit, ever available
for God to use.

Illustration

If you are a person of average size, you perform in each day of 24 hours the following functions: your heart beats 103,689 times; your blood travels 168,000,000 miles. You breathe 23,040 times; you inhale 438 cubic feet of air. You eat between 3 and 4 pounds of food, and drink 3 quarts of liquid, and perspire about 2 pints through your skin; your body maintains a steady temperature of 98.6 degrees under all weather conditions. You generate 450 foot tons of energy; you speak 4,800 words (men only), and move and use over 700 muscles, use 7,000,000 brain cells, and walk 7 miles (women only in the home—not men). And this body belongs to God. With all this activity, how much of it is dedicated to the Creator? . . . Make it a present to God today.[2]

Having presented our bodies "a living sacrifice" to God, let us take time to thank him for them. Dr. Alton Ochsner of New Orleans, Louisiana, a distinguished physician, has said it well in an uplifting prayer entitled:

My Body

Thank you, God, for this body.
For the things it can feel—
The things it can sense,
Thank you for the wondrous things it can do.
For the bright figure of my body at the day's begin-
    ning.
For its weariness at the day's end.
Thank you even for its pain—
If only to sting me into awareness of my own
    existence upon Earth.
I look upon your creation in amazement.
For we are indeed fearfully and wonderfully made.
All its secret, silent machinery—the meshing and
    churning—
What a miracle of design!
Don't let me hurt it, God,

Or scar it, or spoil it,
Or overindulge or overdrive it.
But don't let me coddle it, either, God.
Let me love my body enough to keep it agile.
And able, and well, and strong.

B. Physically Happy

". . . with bright eyes" (16:12); "a lad with fine eyes"
(Moffatt). This is a phrase which beautifully expresses
the sparkle, alertness, and vitality which twinkle in the
eyes of one who is physically healthy and happy. How
many Christians fall short of this standard! Nor can this
fact be attributed necessarily to suffering and physical
weakness. Rather, it is often those who suffer excruci-
ating pain who show forth the glory, joy, and radiance of
the Lord Jesus. Their very suffering has enriched their
spiritual experience, and this is reflected in their coun-
tenance. There should be a glow and a radiance about
our appearance, witnessing to our physical and spiritual health. When Stephen appeared before the coun-
cil to answer charges of blasphemy it is reported that
all who looked ". . . steadfastly at him saw his face as
the face of an angel" (Acts 6:15). The glory of the Lord
shone through his physical appearance.

Illustration

It is related that one day Charles Finney looked at a
scoffer, and the scoffer got saved; such was the power of
the Spirit in a sanctified life. It is said that Evan Roberts
used to look around an assembly, and souls came under
conviction; such was the flow of the Spirit's power through
a clean channel. How much of the Spirit-filled look is radi-
ated through our faces?

C. Physically Handsome

". . . he was . . . good-looking" (16:12). The term *handsome* does not convey merely the thought of attractive-

ness. There is a sense in which a person can be attractive without being handsome. To be handsome means to be physically well-proportioned and looked after. How many Christians could look better if only they cared for themselves in a sensible and disciplined manner. Listen to Paul's testimony on this point: ". . . I discipline my body and bring it into subjection, lest when I have preached to others, I myself should become disqualified" (1 Cor. 9:27). The apostle likens the subjection of his body to discipline and mastery with that of athletes and fighters in the Olympic Games. He says, ". . . everyone who competes for the prize is temperate in all things . . ." (1 Cor. 9:25). If these athletes did it for a crown of laurel leaves, how much more should we strive for an incorruptible crown? Whatever else this meant for the apostle, it certainly involved a constant concern. Indeed, he states that care in this realm of his life determined whether or not he was finally approved or disapproved at the judgment seat of Christ.

A surrendered Christian has yielded not only his spirit and soul, but also his body. That is the whole significance of Paul's appeal in Romans 12:1 where he says, "I beseech you therefore, brethren, by the mercies of God, that you present your bodies a living sacrifice, holy, acceptable to God, which is your reasonable service."

Conclusion

These qualities of character, capability, and comeliness are within the possibility of everyone; they are the result of the man or woman who is prepared to yield spirit, soul, and body unreservedly to the Holy Spirit. Only when God discovers a man or woman who will do this does he anoint them for specific service.

Having discovered his man, God commanded Samuel to fill his horn with oil, single out David among his brethren, and pour the oil of anointing upon his head. It was not until some years later that David fully realized all that for which God had apprehended him. At the same time, having been set apart by anointing, David knew that God had a great future for him and quietly and obediently waited for the gradual unfolding of his will.

God is still looking for men and women who he can set apart for some specific service. What is he going to discover as he comes to our lives? Oh, that our prayer might be:

> Lord, make me useful to Thee,
> Send now Thy Spirit to me;
> Thy perfect will, in me fulfill,
> Lord, make me useful to Thee.[3]
>   E. H. G. Sargent

How God Distinguishes His Man
1 Samuel 17:1–51, 57–58

"David prevailed over the Philistine with a sling and a stone, and struck the Philistine and killed him. But there was no sword in the hand of David" (17:50).

Introduction

When God has discovered his man he distinguishes him. In other words, he brings him into relief against the background of others. He points him out publicly as the man after his own heart. There are three ways in particular in which God distinguishes his man, and we shall see them as we follow God's dealings with David in this chapter.

I. God Distinguished David by Employing Him

"Then David said to Saul, 'Let no man's heart fail because of him; your servant will go and fight with this

Philistine'" (17:32). The significance of this becomes
apparent when we realize that David was employed at a
time when everyone else was failing God for fear of the
enemy. Apart from David, there was no one on whom God
could lay his hand; so once again David is marked out as a
man after God's own heart.

Notice how God's employment of David distinguished
him as:

A. Ready for Any Call

Recall three statements in this connection: verse 15:
". . . David . . . returned from Saul to feed his father's
sheep at Bethlehem"; verse 17: ". . . Jesse said to . . .
David, . . . 'run to your brothers at the camp'"; verse 32:
". . . David said . . . 'your servant will go and fight with
this Philistine.'" It did not matter what the call was—
to feed sheep, to find his brothers, or to fight the Philistine: David was ready. The apostle Paul has beautiful
expectations of women who are true helpers in the life
of the church. He says that they are to be ". . . faithful in
all things" (1 Tim. 3:11). This was David. Like the motto
"R.F.A." in the British Army during World War II, David
was "ready for anything." What a challenge to us!

B. Ready for Any Circumstance

". . . David rose early in the morning, . . . and went
as Jesse had commanded him" (17:20). There is nothing to indicate that David knew what lay before him on
that memorable day; but in spite of this he was not
taken by surprise. As a man of God, he had learned how
to react to any circumstance. This is why God employed
him. The true test of "quality Christianity" is not only
action, but *reaction*. It is the ability to react to any situation as Jesus would react. How do we react to circumstances which happen to be outside of our plans?

C. Ready for Any Cost

"Then David said to Saul, 'Let no man's heart fail because of him; your servant will go and fight with this Philistine'" (17:32). When David told Saul that God would deliver him out of the hand of the Philistine (17:37) he was not presuming on God; rather, he was resting in the will of God. If the encounter with Goliath meant death for him he was prepared to pay the price; on the other hand, if it meant deliverance, David was just as ready.

How does this compare with our lives? Can we look into the face of the risen Savior and say, "Anywhere, at any time, at any cost, Lord"? When God employs a man he enables him.

Illustration

It was Dwight L. Moody who said, "I am only one, but I am one. I cannot do everything, but I can do something. And that which I can do, by the grace of God, I will do." With that simple commitment he became a great and effective preacher and evangelist. Through his campaigns in England, Ireland, Scotland, and America, God used his ministry to bring revival to both sides of the Atlantic. It is said that Moody traveled more than one million miles, addressed more than one hundred million persons, and personally dealt with nearly seven hundred and fifty thousand individuals. Despite his meager education he became a noted educator and builder of schools; in particular, Moody Bible Institute, the first Bible school of its kind in this country.

II. God Distinguished David by Enabling Him

"Then David said to the Philistine, 'You come to me with a sword, with a spear, and with a javelin. But I come to you in the name of the LORD of hosts, the God of the armies of Israel, whom you have defied. This day the LORD will deliver you into my hand, and I will strike you and take your head from you. And this day I will give the carcasses of the camp of the Philistines to the birds of the air and the wild beasts of the earth, that all the earth may know that there is a God in Israel. Then all this assembly shall know that the LORD does not save with sword and spear; for the battle is the LORD's and he will give you into our hands'" (17:45–47).

David was still very young and, humanly speaking, was not equal to what was demanded of him. However, David had long learned that "little is much when God is in it." This was summed up in his words, ". . . I come . . . in the name of the LORD of Hosts . . ." (17:45). With the Lord of hosts, David knew that he was always in the majority. With God's enabling grace:

A. He Fought Dissuasive Cowardice

"And all the men of Israel, when they saw the man, fled from him and were dreadfully afraid" (17:24). David's answer to this was one of God-enabled *courage*; ". . . who is this uncircumcised Philistine, that he should defy the armies of the living God?" (17:26).

Solomon tells us that "the fear of man brings a snare . . ." (Prov. 29:25). This is illustrated again and again throughout the Scriptures. Without doubt, it was largely because of the fear of man that Peter denied his Lord. He was scared lest he should be found to be one of the disciples. It was ". . . for fear of the Jews . . ." that the disciples locked themselves in the Upper Room (John 20:19). Cowardice is a very real problem that has to be faced and overcome by the divine enabling—if a person is ever to be used by God. One of the evidences of the anointing of the Holy Spirit in the early church was that the apostles could speak with boldness. God grant us to know a courage similar to David's as we learn to count on the enabling of the Holy Spirit.

Illustration

In 1953 a columnist of the *Chicago News* by the name of Harris, a man who acquired a large reader following by his frank and often caustic comments, wrote what he called "A Prayer for the President"—"O Lord . . . give him the courage, not of his convictions, but of your commandments."[1]

Not a bad prayer to pray for any leader!

B. He Fought Destructive Criticism

". . . Eliab his oldest brother . . . said, 'Why did you come down here? And with whom have you left those few sheep in the wilderness? I know your pride and the insolence of your heart, for you have come down to see the battle'" (17:28). David's answer to this was one of God-enabled *challenge*: "'What have I done now? Is there not a cause?'" (17:29).

A subtle method which the devil employs for paralyzing Christian witness is that of destructive criticism. We are so familiar with that hurtful approach of Eliab, which insinuates that our service for Christ is nothing more than personal conceit, pride, or even self-expressionism. But David's reply was as sound as it was shattering. He could sincerely say that there was a deeper cause than mere curiosity or interest. The honor and glory of God had been brought into question, and it was his duty to answer that challenge.

What effect has destructive criticism on our inner convictions and determination to stand true to what we know to be the true evangelical cause?

C. He Fought Deflective Concern

"And Saul said to David, 'You are not able to go against this Philistine to fight with him; for you are but a youth, and he a man of war from his youth'" (17:33). David's answer to this was one of God-enabled *confi-*

dence: ". . . The LORD . . . will deliver me from the hand of this Philistine . . ." (17:37).

Once again, this represents a cunning approach of the devil. There is the fatherly, or sometimes motherly, concern shown for our protection and welfare, which is nothing more than an attempt to deflect us from the path of duty.

How dramatically this is illustrated in the life of our Lord, when Peter—with a perfectly legitimate and human concern—attempted to persuade the Master from walking the way of the cross. Jesus had been showing his disciples how that he must go to Jerusalem and ". . . suffer many things from the elders and chief priests and scribes, and be killed, and be raised again the third day." Then we read that Peter ". . . took him aside and began to rebuke him, saying, 'Far be it from you, Lord; this shall not happen to you!' But he turned and said to Peter, 'Get behind me, Satan! You are an offense to me, for you are not mindful of the things of God, but the things of men'" (Matt. 16:21–23).

Like the Lord Jesus, David was confident that God had called him to face the giant Goliath, and that—if it were his will—he was able to deliver him out of the hand of the Philistine. To the Israelites, Goliath was "too big to hit"; but to little David, he was "too big to miss."

D. He Fought Depressive Competence

"And the Philistine said to David, 'Come to me, and I will give your flesh to the birds of the air and the beasts of the field!'" (17:44). David's answer to this was one of God-enabled *conquest*; "So David prevailed over the Philistine with a sling and a stone . . ." (17:50).

The stature, armor, and manner of Goliath could have had a devastating effect on David, had he not been assured of the victory which is available to those who rely on God in simple trust. God's answer was victory for his servant with a mere sling and stone.

When the apostle Paul points out to us the enemy of our souls he uses language which could be quite terrifying. He says, ". . . we do not wrestle against flesh and blood, but against principalities, against powers, against the rulers of the darkness of this age, against spiritual hosts of wickedness in the heavenly places" (Eph. 6:12). Here is Satan with his myriads of supporters. But in another place, the same apostle reminds us that ". . . the weapons of our warfare are not carnal but mighty in God for pulling down strongholds" (2 Cor. 10:4). Our task is not to pit our strength against the formidable enemy, but rather to ". . . submit to God. Resist the devil and [see him] flee from [us]" (James 4:7). John puts it in a nutshell when he says, ". . . this is the victory that has overcome the world—our faith" (1 John 5:4).

Thus we see again how God distinguished his servant by enabling him to do the impossible. What a tremendous difference it would make in our lives if we really believed that the God who lived in David's day is just the same today! Dissuading influences made no difference to David. His determination was to fulfill all God's will. Having put his hand to the plow he would not look back.

III. God Distinguished David by Exalting Him

"Then, as David returned from the slaughter of the Philistine, Abner took him and brought him before Saul with the head of the Philistine in his hand" (17:57). God always exalts a man who is humble and usable enough to stand the wonder of divine exaltation. What is more, when God exalts a man there are unmistakable marks which demonstrate it:

A. God Is Honored

"When David spoke to the men who stood by him, saying, 'What shall be done for the man who kills this Philistine and takes away the reproach from Israel? For who is this uncircumcised Philistine, that he should defy the armies of the living God?'" (17:26). These words, together with the general trend of the chapter, make it plain that David's real concern was the honor and glory of the Lord; nothing else seemed to matter. This is beautifully summed up when he says, ". . . all this assembly shall know that the LORD does not save with sword and spear; for the battle is the LORD's . . ." (17:47).

B. Others Are Helped

Israel was saved. We read, "Then the children of Israel returned from chasing the Philistines, and they plundered their tents" (17:53).

This is an eternal law. When God exalts a man, the name of the Lord is honored; and from the exalted life flows saving and sanctifying power. A life that is promoted by God becomes a personality which is consciously and unconsciously redemptive.

C. Self Is Hidden

The last verse of this chapter crowns the whole story: "And Saul said to him, 'Whose son are you, young man?' And David answered, 'I am the son of your servant Jesse the Bethlehemite'" (17:58). How incomparably beautiful! A moment's reflection will reveal what David might have said. He could have told of his being chosen from among all his brothers; of his anointing, and of the Spirit of God coming upon him; but, instead, he quietly and naturally hides all of self behind the glory of the Lord.

This, then, is the threefold mark of the man whom God has exalted. God is honored, others are helped, and self is hidden.

Illustration

In conversation with Professor S. F. B. Morse, the inventor of the telegraph, the Rev. George W. Hervey asked this question: "Professor Morse, when you were making your experiments . . . in your room in the university, did you ever come to a [standstill], not knowing what to do next?" "Oh, yes, more than once." "And at such times what did you do next?" "I may answer you in confidence, sir," said the professor, "but it is a matter of which the public knows nothing. I prayed for more light." "And the light generally came?" "Yes, and may I tell you that when flattering honors came to me from America and Europe on account of the invention which bears my name, I never felt I deserved them. I had made a valuable application of electricity, not because I was superior to other men, but solely because God, who meant it for mankind, must reveal it to someone, and was pleased to reveal it to me." In view of these facts, it is not surprising that the inventor's first message was, "What hath God wrought!"[2]

Conclusion

We have seen in our study that God distinguishes his man by employing him, enabling him, and exalting him. Have we proved this in our lives, or are we too unready to be employed, too unwilling to be enabled, and too unusable to be exalted? God grant that we might come to the place where we can pray:

> O use me, Lord, use even me,
> Just as Thou wilt, and when, and where;
> Until Thy blessed face I see,
> Thy rest, Thy joy, Thy glory share.
> Frances R. Havergal

4

How God Develops His Man
1 Samuel 18:1–5, 15, 30

"The soul of Jonathan was knit to the soul of David, and Jonathan loved him as his own soul" (18:1).

Introduction

There can be no full-orbed development of personality without social life. For this reason God has graciously given to man the gift of friendship.

This was true in the case of David. Indeed, such was the level and lastingness of his friendship with Jonathan that it has come to be recognized as one of the most beautiful illustrations of God's purpose in human friendship. In the verses before us, we learn how God developed David through:

I. The Attraction of Friendship

"And it was so, when he [David] had finished speaking to Saul that the soul of Jonathan was knit to the soul of David, and Jonathan loved him as his own soul" (18:1).

This was a development which was mainly *personal.* It was after Jonathan had witnessed David's behavior before Saul, following the slaying of the giant, Goliath, that his soul went out to David. Such physical attraction always makes an impact on the physical natures involved. In the case of David:

A. It Developed a Sense of Being Personally Watched

". . . David went out wherever Saul sent him, and behaved wisely. . . . Therefore, when Saul saw that he behaved very wisely, he was afraid of him. . . . David behaved more wisely than all the servants of Saul, so that his name became highly esteemed" (18:5, 15, 30). There is no man with physical good taste who does not become disciplined and developed through a sense of being watched. From a Christian point of view, this is of utmost importance. What we are in spirit and soul will be interpreted to the world by the way we behave. This is why the apostle commands us to ". . . walk circumspectly, not as fools but as wise" (Eph. 5:15); and again: "Walk in wisdom toward those who are outside . . ." (Col. 4:5). We can only achieve this standard of behavior when we are careful to ". . . glorify God in [our bodies] . . ." (1 Cor. 6:20).

B. It Developed a Sense of Being Personally Wanted

". . . Jonathan, Saul's son, delighted much in David" (1 Sam. 19:1). Try to imagine what it must have meant to David, the farmer's son, to feel that he was wanted as a friend of the heir to the throne! There is nothing more exhilarating than this. It even makes a difference in the personal appearance of the person who is made aware that he or she is wanted as a friend; it makes them radiant. How true this is of the highest friendship of all! Every Christian knows something of the transforming

friendship of Jesus, when ". . . with unveiled face,
beholding as in a mirror the glory of the Lord, [he is]
being transformed into the same image from glory to
glory, just as by the Spirit of the Lord" (2 Cor. 3:18).

Illustration

In olden time there reigned in Persia a great monarch,
Shah Abbis, who loved his people. To know them more perfectly he used to mingle with them in various disguises.
One day he went as a poor man to the public baths, and
there in the tiny cellar he sat beside the fireman who
tended the furnace. At mealtime he shared his coarse food
and talked to the lonely man as a friend. Again and again
he visited him until the man grew to love him. Then one
day he told him he was the Emperor, and he waited for the
man to ask some gift from him. But the fireman sat gaz-
ing on him with love and wonder, and at last he spoke:
"You left your palace and your glory to sit with me in this
dark place, to partake of my coarse fare, to care whether
my heart is glad or sorry. On others you may bestow rich
presents, but to me you have given yourself; and it only
remains to pray that you never withdraw the gift of your
friendship."[1]

C. It Developed a Sense of Being Personally Worthy

"And Jonathan took off the robe that was on him and
gave it to David, with his armor, even to his sword and
his bow and his belt" (18:4). You will remember that
David refused to wear Saul's armor when it was offered
him to fight Goliath. His language was, ". . . I cannot
walk with these, for I have not tested them . . ." (1 Sam.
17:39). The reason he refused the king's military dress
was because he had not yet proved himself worthy of
the friendship of the royal house; but after slaying
Goliath he felt quite different about it. The friendship
which sprang up between Jonathan and himself developed that sense of being worthy now to don the apparel
and armor of Prince Jonathan. If he had earned a place at

all in the king's palace, then he must walk worthily of that high vocation.

Similarly, if our friendship with the Lord Jesus and his people is genuine, then we, too, should ". . . walk worthy of the calling with which [we] were called" (Eph. 4:1). Only through the enrichment of such sanctifying friendship can we ever be made to feel worthy, for in ourselves we are totally unworthy and unprofitable.

We see, then, how personal development was enhanced through the attraction of friendship. In the same way, Christian fellowship ought to have an impact upon us. Our appearance and demeanor ought to express something of the purifying and beautifying effect of Christian friendship.

II. The Affinity of Friendship

". . . the soul of Jonathan was knit to the soul of David . . ." (18:1).

This was a development which was mainly *psychological*.

The word *knit* means "to bend by drawing closer and closer." This knitting was effected in the realm of the soul, which is the seat of the mind, heart, and will. This affinity of soul developed:

A. The Mind, or the Intellectual Life

Solomon tells us that "as iron sharpens iron, so a man sharpens . . . his friend" (Prov. 27:17). Nothing develops the mind more than mental stimulation; but such stimulation is only possible where there is mental affinity. As part of the human race, each of us is a separate individual, having our own personality and identity; yet we are members of a larger community. The Word of God reminds us, ". . . none of us lives to himself, and no one dies to himself" (Rom. 14:7). We influence others and are, in turn, affected by them. This implies involvement with society, rather than isolation from it. In fact, the Bible tells us, ". . . It is not good that man should be alone . . ." (Gen. 2:18). Solitude rigidly maintained over a long period of time produces insanity. We are told that one half of our human faculties are intended for interaction with others, while the other half is occupied with powers for regulating such social interaction. How important it is, then, that we should know friendship (generally, if not personally), if our minds are to be developed.

Illustration

Thomas A. Edison, the great inventor, was talking one day with the governor of North Carolina, and the governor complimented him on his inventive genius. "I am not a great inventor," said Edison. "But you have over a thousand patents to your credit, haven't you?" queried the governor. "Yes, but about the only invention I can really claim as absolutely original is the phonograph," was the reply. "Why, I'm afraid I don't understand what you mean," said the governor. "Well," explained Edison, "I guess I'm an awfully good sponge. I absorb ideas from every source I can, and put them to practical use. Then I improve them until they become of some value. The ideas which I use are mostly the ideas of other people who don't develop them themselves."[2]

B. The Heart or the Emotional Life

"As in water face [mirrors] face, so a man's heart reveals the man" (Prov. 27:19). There is nothing like heart-to-heart friendship for searching, sanctifying, and satisfying our emotional life. The wise man says, "As in water face [mirrors] face, so a man's heart reveals the man" (Prov. 27:19); that is to say, as my face is reflected in the pool of water, so my heart answers to the heart of my friend. In the language of friendship, this is healthy and strengthening. That is why Solomon reminds us, "Faithful are the wounds of a friend . . ." (Prov. 27:6).

Dinah Craik, in her little book *Life for a Life*, says of friendship: "Oh, the comfort—the inexpressible comfort of feeling safe with a person, having neither to weigh thoughts, nor measure words—but pouring them all right out—just as they are—Chaff and grain together—Certain that a faithful hand will take and sift them—Keep what is worth keeping—And with the breath of kindness blow the rest away." Only heart friendship can produce such understanding and faithfulness as this.

C. The Will or the Volitional Life

Ecclesiastes 4:9–10 reminds us, "Two are better than one, because they have a good reward for their labor. For if they fall, one will lift up his companion. But woe to him who is alone when he falls, for he has no one to help him up." Strength of will is not willfulness, but willingness, and such willingness can only be developed through the experience of deep friendship. When the Lord Jesus said ". . . not my will, but yours, be done" (Luke 22:42) it was because He had ". . . learned obedience by the things which he suffered" (Heb. 5:8).

The friendship between David and Jonathan was such that Jonathan could say to him, "Whatever you yourself desire, I will do it for you" (1 Sam. 20:4).

Our volitional life can never be developed through the willfulness of individualism. We can only be strong in the realm of our wills as we submit to the sovereignty of Christ and the friendship of fellow believers. This lays an importance upon personal friendship as well as on our relationship to and responsibility within the church of Jesus Christ.

III. The Affection of Friendship

"Then Jonathan and David made a covenant, because he loved him as his own soul" (18:3).
This was a development which was mainly *spiritual*. Affection, in its purer sense, always elevates until it develops:

A. A Spiritual Life

". . . Jonathan and David made a covenant . . ." (18:3). The word "covenant" denotes a mutual agreement. Such covenants of brotherhood or friendship were common in the East and were an outward token of a common life upon which the covenanters had embarked. David and Jonathan had agreed that their lives were going to be lived not only for God, but in God; so they made what they called ". . . a covenant of the LORD . . ." (1 Sam. 20:8). In that same chapter (verse 16) we read that ". . . Jonathan made [or cut] a covenant with the house of David. . . ." This indicates that each man bared his arm and made an incision, mingling the blood, thus sealing their friendship in Jehovah their God. What a level of friendship this was!

Illustration

Soon after Jack Benny died, George Burns, the quintessential song and dance man, was interviewed on a TV talk show. When asked about his relationship to Jack, George flicked his unlit cigar and answered with that distinctive voice so experienced in delivering punchy lines, "Well," he said, "Jack and I had a wonderful friendship for nearly fifty-five years; Jack never walked out on me when I sang a song, and I never walked out on him when he played the violin." Though couched in jest, Burns expressed the fact of commitment. He and Benny were genuinely close friends—committed friends. While they were not given to a formal covenant, hardly a day went by when they didn't talk, at least by telephone. Each would have done anything for the other. People who knew them envied their commitment. Reciprocal commitment does not require a formal covenant, although in the biblical friendship of Jonathan and David, such a pact existed (1 Sam. 20:16–17). In fact, one does not know early in most relationships if and when the blossom of commitment will occur, but there is no doubt about its beauty and fragrance once it bursts forth.[3]

If we are to know a friendship which is deep and indissoluble, it must be in the Lord and on the basis of blood that was shed at Calvary. Only this kind of friendship will develop our spiritual life. The test of true affection can always be based on whether friendship leads to spirituality or carnality.

B. A Spiritual Love

"Jonathan . . . loved him as his own soul" (18:3). When the affection of friendship leads to spiritual life it is transformed into divine love. No longer is it the sentimental, sickly affection of sinful men and women, but rather the love that never faileth. This is why David lamented, in later years, over the death of Jonathan with these words: "Your love to me was wonderful, surpassing the love of women" (2 Sam. 1:26).

Spiritual love is sacrificial love, and this is beautifully illustrated in Jonathan's love for David. First Samuel 18:4 tells us that ". . . Jonathan took off the robe that was on him and gave it to David, with his armor, even to his sword and his bow and his belt." Sacrificial love is always ready to surrender its rights, responsibilities, and riches for others. In the passage before us we see Jonathan sacrificing:

1. HIS RIGHTS IN THE INTERESTS OF FRIENDSHIP WITH DAVID

"Jonathan took off the robe that was on him . . . with his armor. . ." (18:4). The cloak or robe was the insignia of his princely life in the palace, while his

armor speaks of his professional life. Whatever rights
he had as a prince or professional soldier were now
willingly surrendered to David.

2. HIS RESPONSIBILITIES IN THE INTERESTS OF FRIENDSHIP WITH DAVID

". . . Jonathan . . . gave . . . to David . . . his sword
and his bow . . ." (18:4). These were the weapons of
warfare and represented his responsibilities as second only to his father, the king. The act of handing
them over to David was highly significant. As friends,
they now shared both the responsibilities and the
honors.

3. HIS RICHES IN THE INTERESTS OF FRIENDSHIP WITH DAVID

". . . Jonathan . . . gave . . . David . . . his belt" (18:4).
The military belt was the chief ornament of a soldier
and highly prized. It was a rich present, a token of
remembrance. Belts were only worn by the wealthy
and were of costly materials. Indeed, they were often
used as pockets for money and jewels; therefore, they
represented wealth. True love and friendship always
share wealth in the interests of the one loved. What a
sacred and purifying power such love can be in Christian friendship!

C. A Spiritual Loyalty

"So Jonathan made a covenant with the house of
David, saying, 'Let the LORD require it at the hand of
David's enemies.' And Jonathan again caused David to
vow, because he loved him; for he loved him as he loved
his own soul" (1 Sam. 20:16–17). Even though this
friendship between David and Jonathan incurred the
danger of death from Saul and his servants, they continued to be loyal to one another, right to the end of
their days. When they had to separate from each other,
Jonathan could say to David, ". . . Go in peace, since we

have both sworn in the name of the LORD, saying, 'May the LORD be between you and me, and between your descendants and my descendants forever' . . ." (1 Sam. 20:42). We see how friendship developed a loyalty which neither danger nor death can destroy.

Indeed, the history of the church reveals that when the friendship of Christian people has developed into spiritual loyalty, no amount of persecution or peril can separate believing people from the Lord or from one another. It was the Savior himself who said, "By this all will know that you are my disciples, if you have love for one another" (John 13:35).

Illustration

When Confederate spy Sam Davis was captured, he was found to possess some important papers of great value to the Union Army. The officers knew that, ultimately, he was not responsible for having those papers, so as he stood blindfolded before a firing squad, he was given a final chance for reprieve. The officer in charge said to him, "If you will give us the name of the man who furnished you this information, you may go free." He refused, saying, "If I had a thousand lives I would give them all before I would betray a friend." Here was true friendship.[4]

Conclusion

We have seen how God develops his man through the attraction, affinity, and affection of friendship. Such friendship, in the highest sense, is the gift of God for the development of human personality. We should see to it that we use, and not abuse, this priceless gift, developing the physical, psychological and spiritual part of our beings until there is real life, love, and loyalty in the Lord.

5

How God Delivers His Man
1 Samuel 20

"Come to the place where you hid on the day of the deed; and remain by the stone Ezel" (20:19).

Introduction

In terms of spiritual experience, David, in this chapter, had reached a point which paralleled Paul's conflict in Romans 7. There Paul cries, "O wretched man that I am! Who will deliver me from this body of death?" (Rom. 7:24). This was precisely David's concern. He says, ". . . there is but a step between me and death" (20:3). The "body of death," for David, was represented by Saul, the man of the flesh. David had to decide whether he would be mastered by the body of death, or learn God's way of victory and deliverance. This crisis was the inevitable result of David's development in the things of God. The issue plainly was Saul or God. David decided for God against Saul, and in the verses before us we have the story of how God delivered his man. The stages of this deliverance could be set out as follows:

I. Price of Deliverance

". . . there is but a step between me and death" (20:3). David had reached the point where he had to count the cost.

A. There Was the Price of Laxity

"Then David fled from Naioth in Ramah, and went and said to Jonathan, 'What have I done? What is my iniquity, and what is my sin before your father, that he seeks my life?'" (20:1). From this and other verses we see that the price of laxity, for David, was a return to Saul, who represented life in the flesh. To go back to him would have appeared to be popular and exceedingly brave, but, in the last analysis, would have involved a compromising laxity which would have led to the defeat of God's purpose for David.

What a lesson to those of us who want to pander to Saul, the man of the flesh! The commentary of the New Testament on such an attitude, is extremely solemn and searching. The apostle Paul says: ". . . to be carnally minded is death, . . . because the carnal mind is enmity against God; for it is not subject to the law of God, nor indeed can be. So then, those who are in the flesh cannot please God" (Rom. 8:6–8). And again: ". . . if you live according to the flesh you will die . . ." (Rom. 8:13). Galatians 6:8 adds: ". . . he who sows to his flesh will of the flesh reap corruption . . ." (Gal. 6:8).

Illustration

When the Bastille, a castle-like prison in Paris, was about to be destroyed in 1789, a convict was brought out who had been confined in one of its gloomy cells for many years.

But instead of joyfully welcoming his liberty, he begged to
be taken back. It had been a long time since he had seen
the sunshine; [consequently], his eyes could not endure
its brightness. His only desire was to die in the murky dungeon where he had been a captive. In the same way, some
men . . . become so hardened in their sin that they prefer
the dark ways of eternal death.[1]

B. There Was the Price of Victory

"Then Jonathan said to David: The LORD God of Israel
is witness! When I have sounded out my father some-
time tomorrow, or the third day, and indeed there is
good toward David, and I do not send to you and tell
you, may the LORD do so and much more to Jonathan.
But if it pleases my father to do you evil, then I will
report it to you and send you away, that you may go in
safety. And the LORD be with you as he has been with
my father" (20:12–13). The price of victory, for David,
meant leaving Saul once for all, and cleaving to his God.
This would appear outwardly unpopular and cowardly.
Ultimately, however, it would mean deliverance from
all that would frustrate God's purpose for David. What a
challenge this brings! Are we prepared to pay the price
of victory?

Once again, the New Testament has something to say
about this approach in the Christian experience: ". . . if
by the Spirit you put to death the deeds of the body, you
will live" (Rom. 8:13). David could have argued that,
having faced Goliath, he was surely able to confront a
cowardly king like Saul; but this would have been act-
ing in the flesh. God, who had protected his life from
Goliath's spear, could not shield his servant from the
consequences of operating with such carnal-mindedness.

We, too, can overcome our Goliaths in the power of
the Spirit; but to act in the energy of the flesh is to fail
tragically and fatally. Every course of action, therefore,
must be weighed carefully, in terms of the price of laxity

or victory. David counted the cost and was prepared to go through with God.

Illustration

The story is told of a rising young physician in one of our larger cities who had a successful practice, earning thousands of dollars a year. One day he walked into the office of a missionary organization and laid down his application before the board for appointment as a medical missionary. Dumbfounded, the Board asked him if he had carefully considered this action and what it would cost him. He replied he was doing what he felt God had led him to do. They asked him if he knew what salary he might expect as a missionary if he were given the appointment, and he said he did. It would be $50.00 a month for himself, the same amount for his wife, and a smaller amount for his two children. He was accepted and became one of the great medical missionaries of this generation. Position and salary, comfort and convenience, did not count with him, once he had committed everything to God, desiring only to live for his glory.[2]

II. The Place of Deliverance

". . . come to the place where you hid on the day of the deed; and remain by the stone Ezel" (20:19). God never leaves his people in any doubt as to the place of deliverance. Indeed, there is only one such place, and that is Calvary's cross. How beautifully this is typified and foreshadowed in the story before us. Jonathan (whose name means "the gift of God") leads David to the stone Ezel—the place of deliverance. The significance of this becomes apparent when we discover that:

A. The Stone Marked the Place of Decision

". . . the place where you hid on the day of the deed [the day of the business] . . ." (20:19). David had transacted business at this spot before (see 19:1–3), and on that occasion had experienced deliverance, but now Jonathan leads him back for a deeper experience.

In a similar way, God calls us back to the cross. It is only at the cross that decisions are made. It is only at the cross that we can know deliverance over the "Saul" who would master our lives. In terms of a spiritual principle, we hear the echo of this truth in the Epistle to the Romans: "knowing this, that our old man was crucified with him, that the body of sin might be done away with, that we should no longer be slaves of sin. For he who has died has been freed from sin" (Rom. 6:6–7).

Illustration

He was a long, lanky, ungainly backwoodsman from "up-country" who had come down the mighty Mississippi aboard a barge that was loaded with produce for the markets of New Orleans. And now he was walking along the docks taking in the sights. Suddenly he was aware of a crowd that stood close together, listening to the strident voice of an auctioneer. Out of curiosity he approached the group, and to his horror saw that they were auctioning off a number of slaves. He saw them sell a man to one master and his wife to another, saw them tear children from the arms of their parents, and he lifted a long muscular arm toward Heaven and made a vow: "God helping me, someday I'll strike a deathblow to that traffic in lives." God heard that vow, and later on he gave Abraham Lincoln the opportunity to fulfill it. On the cross of Calvary Jesus was fulfilling a vow he had made long before to strike an eternal deathblow to sin and all it stands for, to release anyone from its hellish fetters. The Father, having heard that vow, paved the way for its fulfillment, and then veiled his face in darkness when the hour of Christ's agony came.[3]

B. The Stone Marked the Place of Direction

". . . the stone Ezel" (20:19). Its very name, according to the marginal rendering, means "the place that showeth the way." What the stone meant to David is what the cross means to us today. We cannot attend the drama that was enacted there without following Christ from the cross to the grave, and up to the throne, where he now sits as the risen, all-powerful and glorious Lord. It is as we face these great facts of our faith that we learn our directions for living. ". . . He died for all, that those who live should live no longer for themselves, but for him who died for them and rose again" (2 Cor. 5:15); and once more: "I have been crucified with Christ; it is no longer I who live, but Christ lives in me; and the life which I now live in the flesh I live by faith in the son of God, who loved me and gave Himself for me" (Gal. 2:20).

C. The Stone Marked the Place of Detachment

Speaking of the stone Ezel, where David was commanded to hide, Jonathan said, "I will shoot three arrows to the side of it, as though I shot at a target; and there I will send a lad, saying, 'Go, find the arrows.' If I expressly say to him, 'Look, the arrows are on this side of you; get them and come'—then, as the LORD lives, there is safety for you and no harm. But if I say thus to the young man, 'Look, the arrows are beyond you'—go your way, for the LORD has sent you away" (20:20–22).

Jonathan had planned with David to shoot the arrows before or beyond the stone. Arrows before the stone meant peace with Saul; arrows beyond the stone meant separation from Saul and his worldly kingdom. How significant that arrows beyond left the stone Ezel between the distance covered.

So the believer finds that if he is going to live the detached life of separation to God the cross must come between. Paul refused to ". . . glory except in the cross of our Lord Jesus Christ, by whom the world [had] been crucified to [him], and [he] to the world" (Gal. 6:14). In the light of the cross, the place of deliverance calls for decision, direction, and detachment. To know such deliverance in our lives we must be able to say:

> Jesus, I my cross have taken,
>   All to leave and follow Thee;
> Destitute, despised, forsaken,
>   Thou, from hence, my all shalt be:
> Perish every fond ambition,
>   All I've sought, and hoped, and known;
> Yet how rich is my condition,
>   God and heaven are still my own!
>   Henry P. Lyte

Amplification

Dr. Alan Redpath, in his book on the life of David, points out that at times, under the pressure of some trial, God purposely shoots an arrow from heaven beyond us to take us out into some great destiny for our lives. He writes that in such a situation we have ". . . to be still and wait . . . You have leaned upon Christian friends, seeking their counsel in prayer. You have agonized and wept and prayed. You have tried to hold on to the immediate circumstances, for your heart clings to the familiar, to the beloved, to the things around you with their promise of shelter and security. But the arrow has landed on target beyond you—perhaps because God has called you to some far distant surroundings, or it may be because he will leave you where you are. The message of the arrow beyond you is not primarily geographical, it is spiritual. To all of us today the Lord Jesus is holding out nail-pierced hands and saying, 'Come ye after me, and I make you to become. . . .' And you know what is involved in going onward with him, being poured from vessel to vessel until every prop is stripped from you and you have nothing and nobody upon whom you can depend, except God and his promises. Trust not in the shelter of home and family ties. They will not last, no matter how precious they are. Live sacramentally like broken bread and poured-out wine. Let God empty you out that he may save you from becoming spiritually stale, and lead you ever onward. He is always calling us to pass beyond the thing we know into the unknown. A throne is God's purpose for you; a cross is

God's path for you; faith is God's plan for you. The arrow of God on the target may leave a scar on your heart. In the years to come you may look back upon this time and your eyes fill with tears as you remember the moment when the arrow went beyond. But the Savior is alongside: he is reminding you that the blood which he shed for you, which takes you within the veil—to the place of constant access to his presence—is the blood that takes you outside the camp to the place of consecrated availability for his plan. . . . He has brought you in and sealed you as his own, but now he has shot the arrow beyond you, and he is taking you out."[4]

III. The Path of Deliverance

"Then Jonathan said to David, 'Go in peace, since we have both sworn in the name of the LORD, saying, "May the LORD be between you and me, and between your descendants and my descendants, forever."' So he arose and departed, and Jonathan went into the city" (20:42). From this verse we learn that the path of deliverance is one of:

A. Peace

"Go in peace" (20:42). This is a peace which flows from knowing victory and fellowship in the Lord. It is the peace which passes all understanding. It cannot be explained, but it can be experienced by all who will walk the path of deliverance.

B. Progress

". . . So [David] arose and departed . . ." (20:42). David was not going back to Saul. He was rather going forward into all God's purpose for his life. It is always true that to be in the path of God's deliverance is to be in the path of progress. Peace follows a life of victory; and progress follows a life of peace.

God has called each of us to such a life of advancement and achievement. If we are not progressing it is because we are defeated; there is a fixation point somewhere in our experience. To remain in this condition is to stagnate and to frustrate the fullness of life which God has prepared for all them that love him.

Conclusion

As Christians, we are God's workmanship, created in Christ Jesus for good works, which God has prepared beforehand that we should walk in them (Eph. 2:10). He will not be satisfied unless, and until, we have found, followed, and fulfilled that plan. May we be willing to face the price, place, and path of deliverance so that we will miss nothing that he has intended for our lives.

How God Directs His Man
1 Samuel 23:1–5

"Then David inquired of the Lord . . . And the Lord answered him and said, 'Arise, go . . .'" (23:4).

Introduction

When a man is prepared to walk the path of the will of God he may depend on God's guiding and directing hand, for in the Christian life "a guided way is a guarded way." This fact remains true, whether we consider guidance in its more general aspect or in its particular aspect. It is quite clear that in the general issues of life David trusted God to direct him, using sanctified common sense, but he did not make this the sole basis of guidance when weightier problems were involved, such as the issue he faced in this chapter.

Similarly, in our lives, the witness of sanctified common sense is sufficient for those matters which do not involve grave doubts and uncertainty—provided the believer is experiencing the real joy of abiding in Christ. This is made clear in Proverbs 3:5–6, where the believer is exhorted to "Trust in the LORD with all [his] heart, and lean not on [his] own understanding; in all [his] ways [he is to] acknowledge Him, and He shall direct [his] paths."

There are times, however, when particular direction is required and common-sense judgment is not enough. Accordingly, God has graciously given us principles by which he guides and directs his people, and it is imperative that we should know them. A study of these verses reveals that direction for any given action comes through the agreement of a threefold witness.

In directing David, the man after God's own heart, there was:

I. The Witness of the Circumstantial Signs

"Then they told David, saying, 'Look, the Philistines are fighting against Keilah, and they are robbing the threshing floors.' . . . And David's men said to him, 'Look, we are afraid here in Judah. How much more then if we go to Keilah against the armies of the Philistines?'" (23:1, 3). These circumstantial signs made it obvious to David that he must adopt a line of action. The signs were interpreted through:

A. What Was Seen

". . . the Philistines are fighting against Keilah, and they are robbing the threshing floors" (23:1). Such a state of affairs demanded an answer from David. Action was called for. This fact illustrates how God's direction is usually first suggested. As Christian people, we must keep our eyes open. "Where there is no revelation [or prophetic vision], the people cast off restraint . . ." (Prov. 29:18). Our problem is that we are so often blind to the circumstances around us.

B. What Was Said

"And David's men said to him, 'Look, we are afraid here in Judah. How much more then if we go to Keilah against the armies of the Philistines?'" (23:3). The Philistines were stronger than David the fugitive with his few men; thus creating a situation which called for special thought and procedure.

The warrant of circumstances is one way in which God works today, but it is not sufficient in and of itself. Like David, we must seek further light.

Illustration

Abraham Lincoln was a man who placed great faith in "providential" guidance. Things that he saw during the Civil War were to him a divine mandate which ultimately led to his issuing the Emancipation Proclamation. He said, on one occasion: "If it were not for my belief in an overruling providence, it would be difficult for me, in the midst of such complications, to keep my reason on its seat. But I am confident that the Almighty has his plans and will work them out; and, whether we see it or not, they will be the wisest and best for us. I have always taken counsel of him, and referred to him my plans, and have never adopted a course of proceeding without being assured, as far as I could be, of his approbation. I should be the most presumptuous blockhead . . . if I for one day thought that I could discharge the duties which have come upon me since I came into this place, without the aid and enlightenment of One who is wiser and stronger than all others."[1]

II. The Witness of the Controlling Spirit

"Therefore David inquired of the LORD, saying, 'Shall I go and attack these Philistines?' And the LORD said to David, 'Go and attack the Philistines, and save Keilah'" (23:2). While the Holy Spirit is not specifically mentioned in this verse, it is obvious that the Lord communicated with David—"The LORD said . . ." And as in New Testament times, so in Old Testament times God spoke by his spirit. The evidence that David was being controlled by the Spirit is seen in:

A. His Prayerfulness to Seek the Will of God

"Therefore David inquired of the LORD . . ." (23:2). David sought the Lord's direction concerning the issue which had been raised by the witness of the circumstantial signs. Prayer is an indispensable factor in the understanding of the Lord's will for our lives. He who never prays for direction will never know the certainty and joy of divine guidance.

Illustration

Dr. George Washington Carver was a man of prayer, and in the simplicity of his faith made answered prayer his natural habitat. Someone once asked him if he had ever found prayer for guidance (in connection with his discoveries) to no avail. "Of course not," he said, "That goes without saying. You see, there is no need for anyone to be without direction, or to wander amid the perplexities and complexities of this life. Are we not plainly told, 'In all thy ways acknowledge Him, and He shall direct thy paths'? Why go blundering along on our poor, blind way when God has told us he will help us? God can always be depended upon. Here is a radio. It is little use standing there unless I turn it on and dial the station I want. Then I will have what I seek. It is all so simple; just opening up the avenues of approach to God through prayer."[2]

B. His Preparedness to Serve the Will of God

". . . Shall I go and attack these Philistines? . . ." (23:2). David did not dictate to God what he wanted to do. Though a man of war, and as happy in battle as out of it, he demonstrated his preparedness to do whatever the Lord commanded him.

The intellectual and spiritual confusion in this matter of guidance is usually due to our unwillingness to do God's will, even when the path of direction has been pointed out. It is important not only to know the will of God but to do it.

Amplification

George Mueller was once asked how he ascertained the will of God. Among other things he said: "I seek at the beginning to get my heart into such a state that it has no will of its own in regard to a given matter. Nine-tenths of the difficulties are overcome when our hearts are ready to do the Lord's will, whatever it may be." When one has reached this point it is relatively easy to discover what his will is.

God's Spirit will always confirm a certain course of action where there is prayerfulness and preparedness of heart. Notice how the conviction of God's direction deepened in David's soul—". . . And the LORD said to David, 'Go and attack the Philistines, and save Keilah'" (23:2). This is the way God works today. He deepens the conviction of his direction by the witness of the Holy Spirit, as we wait in his presence with prayerfulness and preparedness of heart.

But even the witness of circumstances and the controlling Holy Spirit were not sufficient for David; and, indeed, can never be for us. There must be:

III. The Witness of the Confirming Scriptures

"Then David inquired of the LORD once again. And the LORD answered him and said, 'Arise, go down to Keilah. For I will deliver the Philistines into your hand'" (23:4). David went back into the presence of God to await a commanding and confirming word, and he was not disappointed. Notice:

A. The Commanding Word

". . . And the LORD answered him and said, 'Arise, go down to Keilah . . .'" (23:4). This is how God still speaks to us as we read his Word. Without forcing the interpretation or significance of a passage, a command seems to leap out of our reading of God's Word, urging us to do this or that. The light of biblical revelation is not so much the flash of one isolated Bible verse as it is the blaze which seems to shine from the Word in the course of the believer's daily devotions and other biblical instruction.

B. The Confirming Word

". . . I will deliver the Philistines into your hand" (23:4). Observe how the word of Scripture only serves to confirm outward circumstances and the inner witness of the Spirit. Here is our assurance of guidance when all three agree. With this David was satisfied. There was nothing left but to obey—whatever the cost. Verse 5 tells what happened: ". . . David and his men went to Keilah and fought with the Philistines, struck them with a mighty blow, and took away their livestock. So David saved the inhabitants of Keilah." God more than honored David's obedience. He became more than conqueror in that given situation.

He'll do the same for us in this day of grace. When God's peace rules in our heart, and the signs, the Spirit, and the Scriptures all witness to a certain line of action, it is imperative that we obey. To disobey is to cancel out the guidance given and to destroy all sense of direction.

The challenge which emerges from this study is just this: Am I, are you, prepared to walk straight ahead when God directs?

Now it is important to point out that the principles of guidance have always been the same. Consider these principles as illustrated in the Old Testament—Example: the children of Israel. They were guided by:

1. THE WITNESS OF CIRCUMSTANTIAL SIGNS

". . . Moses said to Hobab . . . 'We are setting out for the place of which the LORD said, "I will give it to you." Come with us, and we will treat you well: for the LORD has promised good things to Israel. . . . you can be our eyes'" (Num. 10:29–31). Hobab knew the desert like the back of his hand. He was acquainted with all the geography, circumstances, and expected situations of a journey such as the children of Israel were undertaking. His advice, therefore, constituted the witness of circumstantial signs. Moses said, ". . . you can be our eyes" (Num. 10:31).

2. THE WITNESS OF THE CONTROLLING SPIRIT

". . . on the day that the tabernacle was raised up, the cloud covered the tabernacle . . . from evening until morning it was above the tabernacle like the appearance of fire" (Num. 9:15). The pillar of cloud by day, and of fire by night, were the outward symbols of the presence of Jehovah in the camp. In the language of the New Testament, this would represent the Holy Spirit within our bodies. When the pillar of cloud and of fire moved it was the leading from God that the camp should move also.

3. THE WITNESS OF THE CONFIRMING SCRIPTURES

God instructed Moses, saying: "Make two silver trumpets . . . you shall use them for calling the assembly and for directing the movements of the camps" (Num. 10:2). The two trumpets are a beautiful illustration of the commanding and confirming Word of God. When they sounded out across the camp, it was to call the assembly to dismantle their tents and prepare to march.

Now consider these same principles embodied in the New Testament—Example: the children of God. We are guided by:

1. THE WITNESS OF THE CIRCUMSTANTIAL SIGNS

The apostle Paul exhorts us, saying: ". . . do not be unwise, but understand what the will of the Lord is" (Eph. 5:17); and James adds: ". . . you ought to say, 'If the Lord wills, we shall live and do this or that'" (James 4:15).

In practical experience, we see this remarkably illustrated in the vision that came to Paul at night where ". . . A man of Macedonia stood and pleaded with him, saying, 'Come over to Macedonia and help us.' Now after he had seen the vision, immediately we sought to go to Macedonia, concluding that the Lord had called us to preach the gospel to them" (Acts 16:9–10). Dr. Campbell Morgan suggests that the man Paul saw in the vision was none other than Luke. He does not deny that Paul experienced an inner consciousness of a vision of opportunity, but he maintains that we miss the whole value of the story if we try to rob this incident of all the everyday signs with which God seeks to lead his people. Therefore, we should always be on the alert to discern the mind of God in the circumstances and happenings around us.

2. THE WITNESS OF THE CONTROLLING SPIRIT

We read that ". . . as many as are led by the Spirit of God, these are sons of God" (Rom. 8:14). How this is exemplified in the passage in Acts which we have just considered! In verse 6 (Acts 16) we read that the apostle and his companion were ". . . forbidden by the Holy Spirit to preach the word in Asia," and in verse 7 we are told ". . . the Spirit did not permit them" to go into Bithynia. As a result, they concluded that the Spirit was leading them to preach the gospel in Macedonia.

The Holy Spirit will guide the man who is in the attitude in which it is possible for him to be guided. It is an attitude of loyalty to the Lord, faith in the guidance of the Holy Spirit, and constant watchfulness.

Illustration

It is said that a certain guide lived in the deserts of Arabia who never lost his way. He carried with him a homing pigeon with a very fine cord attached to one of its legs. When in doubt as to which path to take, he threw the bird into the air. The pigeon quickly strained at the cord to fly in the direction of home, and thus led the guide accurately to his goal. Because of this unique practice he was known as "the dove man." So, too, the Holy Spirit, the heavenly Dove, is willing and able to direct us in the narrow way that leads to the more abundant life if in humble self-denial we submit to his unerring supervision.[3]

3. THE WITNESS OF THE CONFIRMING SCRIPTURES

David could pray, "Your word is a lamp to my feet and a light to my path" (Ps. 119:105); and again in that same chapter: "Direct my steps by your word . . ." (v. 133). We are reminded in Romans 15:4 that ". . . whatever things were written before were written for our learning, that we through the patience and comfort of the Scriptures might have hope." The Word of God confirms guidance—not so much in the matter of detail as in the matter of duty. No one can be seeking the mind of the Lord and reading the Scriptures regularly without receiving some word of command and confirmation which settles the question of procedure and direction.

Illustration

A man started out through a forest so thickly covered with trees that one day he could not see the sun or sky. After traveling for a long time he knew it was getting night time, so he started for what he thought was home. He was so certain that his direction was right that he did not look at his compass; in fact, he almost threw it away. But when he did look at it, he was surprised to find that he was going west when he thought he was going east. Mentally, he remarked to his compass, "You have never told me an untruth, and I'll trust you now." He followed the compass and came out right. We, too, have a compass that will never tell us an untruth. It is God's Word—the Bible. If we always follow it we will be safe. However, should it tell us something different, even though we think we are right, then let us follow what it says for that is the only safe thing.[4]

Conclusion

God's principles of guidance are eternal. If God's man would be guided, then he must be prepared to bring his will into alignment with God's will. It is only when this is done that the peace of God holds sway over the soul. God make us willing to pray, day by day:

Teach me Thy will, O Lord, Teach me Thy way;
Teach me to know Thy word, Teach me to pray.
Whate'er seems best to Thee, That be my earnest plea,
So that Thou drawest me closer each day.[5]

                                        Katherine A. Grimes

Part 2

Spiritual Secrets: *Elisha*

The Secret of Tragedy
2 Kings 6:1–7

"As one was cutting down a tree, the iron ax head fell into the water" (6:5).

Introduction

Here is a story with deep spiritual and practical lessons. The ax head is the keen cutting edge of a life that is equipped with the power of the Holy Spirit. The loss and recovery of the ax head is an illustrative picture of the manner in which God matches the misery of human tragedy with the miracle of divine victory.

Have you lost your keen cutting edge? Is your witness and service for God ineffective? More importantly, do you know your way back to recovery and power? If you cannot answer these questions in the affirmative then this is a message for you.

To appreciate the personal application of this fascinating Old Testament story, we must observe the significance of:

I. The Loaning of the Ax Head

"It was borrowed" (6:5). With the simple lifestyle of these sons of the prophets, we have every reason to assume that the loaning of the ax head was:

A. The Compassionate Provision of a Benefactor

"It was borrowed" (6:5). This is a lesson we find difficult to learn! We pride ourselves on our accomplishments and achievements and forget to recognize that all that we are and have we owe to the compassionate provision of our heavenly benefactor. The Bible says, "He who did not spare his own Son, but delivered him up for us all, how shall he not with him also freely give us all things?" (Rom. 8:32); and again; "Every good gift and every perfect gift is from above, and comes down from the father of lights, with whom there is no variation or shadow of turning" (James 1:17). So we can say with James M. Gray:

> Naught have I gotten but what I received;
> Grace hath bestowed it since I have believed . . .

Illustration

During his last hours, John Knox woke from a slumber sighing, and told his friends that he had just been tempted to believe that he had "merited heaven and eternal blessedness, by the faithful discharge of my ministry. But blessed be God who has enabled me to beat down and quench the fiery dart, by suggesting to me such passages of Scripture as these: 'What hast thou that thou didst not receive?' 'By the grace of God I am what I am.' 'Not I, but the grace of God which was with me.'"[1]

Now while ". . . the gifts and the calling of God are irrevocable" (Rom. 11:29) he expects an accounting for every talent and ability that he has conferred upon us.

B. The Conditional Provision of a Benefactor

". . . Alas, master! For it was borrowed" (6:5). The very cry of this man indicates that he was under an obligation. Indeed, he was not only responsible for the scheduled task, but accountable for the supplied tool. The story reveals that the training center had become too small, and that further construction was an urgent necessity. To this task the sons of the prophets were now committed. Even so is our obligation in Christian service. God is ever moving on. Where the Spirit is unhindered in evangelistic enterprise there is expansion. For this reason God holds us personally responsible for our tasks and accountable for our tools. By the incoming and infilling of the Holy Spirit every believer is made responsible and accountable to heaven for the way he uses, misuses, or even abuses his time and talents. Oh, that the cry of the prophet's son might be heard more often among us: ". . . Alas, master! For it was borrowed!" (6:5).

Illustration

Daniel Webster, the great statesman of other years, was once asked, "Mr. Webster, what is the most sobering, searching thought that ever entered your mind?" Without hesitancy, the staunch statesman replied, "My personal accountability to God."

II. Losing the Ax Head

"But as one was cutting down a tree, the iron ax head fell into the water . . ." (6:5). Here we face a most solemn warning which we do well to heed. The Spirit of God teaches us here that it is possible to lose our cutting edge, our usefulness, and power for service.

A. It Can Happen While a Person Is Diligent in His Daily Work

"... as one was cutting down a tree, the iron ax head fell into the water . . ." (6:5). This man never lost his ax head through laziness or idleness; he was, perhaps, the busiest man on the work team! What a word this is to all of us! The fact that we are busy in the Lord's service is no final evidence that we are endued with power from on high. Unfortunately, so much Christian activity today is nothing more than noise without power, motion without progress, and show without reality. God have mercy on men and women who try to serve without the Spirit of power and blessing in their lives!

Illustration

John Henry Fabre, the great French naturalist, conducted a most unusual experiment with some Processionary Caterpillars. These caterpillars blindly follow the one in front of them; hence the name. Fabre carefully arranged them in a circle around the rim of a flower pot so that the lead caterpillar actually touched the last one, making a complete circle. In the center of the flower pot he put pine needles, which is the food they eat. The caterpillars started around this circular flower pot. Around and around they went, hour after hour, day after day, night after night. For seven full days and seven full nights they crawled around the flower pot. Finally, they dropped dead of starvation and exhaustion. With an abundance of food less than six inches away they literally starved to death because they confused activity with accomplishment. Many Christians make that same mistake.[2]

B. It Can Happen While a Person Is Negligent in His Daily Watch

"But as one was cutting down a tree, the iron ax head fell into the water . . ." (6:5). This son of a prophet had a mind to work, but had no sense to watch. He was blind to the fact that the ax head was slackening and slipping from the shaft. Tragedy occurred: he lost his ax head in the dark, muddy waters of the Jordan River.

Jesus told his disciples to "Watch and pray, lest [they] enter into temptation . . ." (Mark 14:38). It is a fact that more spiritual breakdown can be traced to a neglected devotional life than to any other cause. Samson lost his power while diligent in working but negligent in watching. His spiritual life began to slip. Then one day he awoke from sleep to go out as before to demonstrate his strength, but ". . . he did not know that the LORD had departed from him" (Judg. 16:20).

Beware of losing your power with God and with men! It can happen while you are diligent in working, yet negligent in watching. The Lord preserve us all!

Illustration

One night some years ago, the captain of a Greenland whaling vessel found himself surrounded by icebergs and "lay-to" till morning, expecting every moment to be ground to pieces. As the morning dawned he sighted a ship not too far away. Getting into a boat with some of his men, he carefully picked his way through the lanes of open ice toward the mysterious-looking craft. Coming alongside, he shouted, "Ship ahoy!" but there was no response. He looked through the porthole and saw a man, evidently the captain, sitting at a table as if writing in a log-book, but the figure was dead and frozen. From the last entry in the log-book it appeared the vessel had been drifting the Arctic seas for thirteen years—a floating sepulchre, manned by a frozen crew. Today there are souls who have refused the divine offer of life, who have forsaken the centers where they were warmed with hallowed influences. As a result they have drifted into the chilling regions of Arctic darkness and frost. Many of these adopt certain appearances of the Christian life, and a name to live by, but are dead![3]

III. Locating the Ax Head

"And the man of God said, 'Where did it fall?' And he showed him the place so he cut off a stick and threw it in there; and he made the iron float" (6:6). Once again, we are confronted with solemn instruction. When the cutting edge is gone and the power is lost, what is the only way of recovery?

If *you* are asking that question then the answer is twofold:

A. The Explanation of the Human Problem

"And the man of God said, 'Where did it fall?' And he showed him the place . . ." (6:6).

The hardest thing for a backslider to do is to explain why he went astray and how he lost his power, but the Lord Jesus, the Man at God's right hand, insists on this. It is a principle of Scripture that *the place of departure is the place of recovery.* You will only find the power where you lost it. It is futile to imagine that you can overlook the past without accounting for it and confessing it before God. The Bible says, ". . . God requires an account of what is past" (Eccles. 3:15); and again: "If we *confess* our sins, he is faithful and just to forgive us our sins and to cleanse us from all unrighteousness" (1 John 1:9). Some people have had to return to sins committed years previously before God restored to them the joy and power of his Spirit.

Where did you lose your power? Show God the place, the time, and the circumstances. Explain to him the problem, for he already knows; nothing is hidden to him. Confession is his way of recovery.

B. The Application of the Divine Power

". . . So he cut off a stick, and threw it in there; and he made the iron float. Therefore he said, 'Pick it up for yourself.' So he reached out his hand and took it." To believe in God is to believe in miracles, and it is obvious that a miracle was performed here. Note the action of the man of God—". . . he cut off a stick . . ." (6:6). The Lord Jesus is often referred to in Scripture as "a Branch" (Isa. 11:1).

The cutting off, of course, speaks of his death. The application of divine power is always the answer to human need. When the message of a crucified Christ is applied to our problems there is *always* release and restoration.

Observe, in our story, that when Elisha cut off the branch and threw it in the river the iron ax head floated to the surface. Here was *liberation.* It not only overcame the law of gravity, but the strength of the current. This reminds us of Paul's words in Romans 8:2: ". . . the law of the Spirit of life in Christ Jesus has made me free from the law of sin and death." The "death" waters of Jordan and the current of the river were no match for the application of divine power. Then there was restoration— ". . . 'Pick it up for yourself.' So he reached out his hand and took it" (6:7).

Thank God, in the cross of Christ there is liberation and restoration for every backslider, every defeated Christian, every fruitless believer. Will you accept God's sentence of death upon your failure and sin and then take his life and power in an act of faith? Power for service can be restored if you are prepared to show God where you lost it, accept the word of the cross, and then take by faith his releasing and restoring life.

Conclusion

We have seen how God can take a life that is lost in the muddy waters of defilement and death and raise it to new life and power. Remember, your ax head is loaned. It can be lost but, thank God, it can be located and recovered.

Although a believer can never lose the person of the Spirit,
he can lose his presence and power. Surely, this is what
William Cowper had in mind when he wrote:

> Return, O holy Dove, return,
> Sweet messenger of rest;
> I hate the sins that made me mourn,
> And drove Thee from my breast.

> The dearest idol I have known,
> Whate'er that idol be,
> Help me to tear it from Thy throne,
> And worship only Thee.

> So shall my walk be close with God,
> Calm and serene my frame;
> So purer light shall mark the road
> That leads me to the Lamb.

The Secret of Misery
2 Kings 4:38–41

"It happened, as they were eating the stew, that they cried out and said, 'O man of God, there is death in the pot!' And they could not eat it" (4:40).

Introduction

Elisha had returned to Gilgal to minister to the sons of the prophets. At the time, there was a famine in the land, and physical distress and spiritual darkness prevailed on every hand. Without doubt, the sons of the prophets felt the effects of the grave conditions then existing. Only when the man of God arrived did the situation began to change. Elisha's arrival represented:

I. God's Sovereign Provision

"And Elisha . . . said to his servant, 'Put on the large pot, and boil stew for the sons of the prophets'" (4:38).

Heaven is never embarrassed by human need. God always has his Elishas who represent the voice of hope in a time of famine. From the dawn of history God has matched human bankruptcy with divine sufficiency, meeting the hunger of men and women at every level. From the story before us we learn that God sovereignly supplied man's needs in terms of:

A. A Purifying Influence

"'Put on the large pot, and boil stew for the sons of the prophets'" (4:38). The seven-year famine that prevailed throughout the country had been predicted by Elisha (see 2 Kings 8:1) and represented the judgment of God upon human sin. But even amid such judgment God was able to provide for the sons of the prophets.

This is a divine principle found throughout Scripture. Recall that when famine threatened the land, in Jacob's day, God had his Joseph to provide corn in Egypt (see Gen. 41). Later on we read that when darkness plagued the Egyptians, the people of God had light in their dwellings (see Exod. 10:21–23). Then think of Elijah who was supplied with food and water by God's raven at the Brook Cherith while the country around him was perishing with hunger (see 1 Kings 17:4–6).

How true are the words: ". . . The LORD will give grace and glory; no good thing will He withhold from those who walk uprightly" (Ps. 84:11). And again David says: "I have been young, and now am old; yet I have not seen the righteous forsaken, nor his descendants begging bread" (Ps. 37:25). Yes, God provides for those who meet his conditions, and in this sense his provision is always a *purifying* influence to his people. Certainly the sons of the prophets would have interpreted such a lesson from the action of Elisha.

Illustration

In his book *Miracles in Black,* Dr. John C. Wengatz tells of an African convert who was left at a new mission station to carry on the Lord's work with a cannibalistic tribe. It was the dry season when Joao Mbaxi took over, but soon the tropical rains would come. Month after month went by but no cloud appeared and people were on the brink of starvation. In all the years they had worshiped their ancient gods, the rains had never failed them. Now Joao was ordered to leave the country and take "the white man's God" with him. He refused. The chief warned him that unless it rained by sunrise the following day they would drink his blood and eat his flesh. Recalling the story of Elijah, Joao went to his hut and prayed with the same fervency as the ancient prophet. Just before daylight thunder was heard in the distance and abundant rain refreshed the entire region. Elijah's God still lives today! As we meet the conditions we will find the Lord pouring out his blessings with the same plenteous supply.[1]

B. A Unifying Influence

"'Put on the large pot . . .'" (4:38). While God's blessings are conditional, his means of supplying the need are always the same. There is only one Calvary, one Pentecost, one Christ. Paul states this well in 1 Corinthians where he says: ". . . we, being many, are one bread and one body; for we all partake of that one bread" (10:17); and again: "For by one Spirit we were all baptized into one body—whether Jews or Greeks, whether slaves or free—and have all been made to drink into one Spirit" (12:13). In Christ our Savior and Sovereign we are always unified.

C. A Satisfying Influence

"'Put on the large pot and boil stew'" (4:38). While all around was death and distress, there was enough

food for the college of the prophets. When God provides
he always satisfies. To appropriate his provision is to
know the satisfaction of our spirits with his life, the satisfaction of our hearts with his love, the satisfaction of
our wills with his freedom, and the satisfaction of our
bodies with his health. How true are the words, "You
open Your hand and satisfy the desire of every living
thing" (Ps. 145:16). The true evidence that we are find-
ing our resources in Christ is that our lives are being
daily purified, unified, and satisfied.

Amplification

Look at the wonder of God's provision: Am I wounded?
He is balm. Am I sick? He is medicine. Am I naked? He is
clothing. Am I poor? He is wealth. Am I hungry? He is bread.
Am I thirsty? He is water. Am I in debt? He is surety. Am I in
darkness? He is sun. Must I face the gathering storm? He
is an anchor. Am I to be tried? He is my advocate. Am I
condemned? He is pardon.[2]

It is often at this point that we spoil the picture and
thwart the purpose of God for our lives, for whereas
Elisha's visit represented God's sovereign provision, his
visit to Gilgal also rebuked:

II. Man's Sinful Intrusion

". . . one went out into the field to gather herbs, and
found a wild vine, and gathered from it a lap full of wild
gourds, and came and sliced them into the pot of stew,
though they did not know what they were. . . . as they
were eating . . . they cried out and said, . . . 'there is death
in the pot'" (4:39–40). It is characteristic of human nature
not only to attempt to improve upon God's provision but to
intrude into God's purpose. We are not told whether the
young prophet of our story acted ignorantly or willfully,
but it seems reasonable to assume that he did not proceed

according to the word of Elisha. How this illustrates the intrusion of self into the purpose of God! Numerous accounts in the Bible demonstrate that wherever self intrudes there is poison in the pot. Think of:

A. The Sinful Intrusion of Adam and Eve for the Sake of Self-Glory

The devil had told Adam and his wife that in the day they ate of the fruit of the garden their eyes would be opened, and they would be ". . . like God, knowing good and evil" (Gen. 3:5). They believed him and ate of the fruit. The New Testament commentary on this episode is very clear: ". . . just as through one man sin entered the world, and death through sin, . . . thus death spread to all men, because all sinned" (Rom. 5:12). Adam's self-intrusion into the purpose and provision of God meant death in the pot. It seems inconceivable that an innocent pair like these two people could wish for anything more than that which God had provided for them in the Garden of Eden; but in response to satanic temptation there was this desire for self-glory, and under pressure the sin was committed, bringing death into the pot.

Illustration

One afternoon Goethe and Beethoven walked together in the Carlsbad Valley to talk at ease. Everywhere, as they walked, passers-by saluted them, pointed them out, and bowed with ostentatious deference. "Isn't it maddening?" exclaimed Goethe. "I simply can't escape this homage." "Don't be too much distressed by it," said Beethoven; "it is just possible that some of it may be for me."[3]

B. The Sinful Intrusion of Nadab and Abihu for the Sake of Self-Effort

In Leviticus 10:1–2 we read: "Then Nadab and Abihu, the sons of Aaron, each took his censer and put fire in it, put incense on it, and offered profane fire before the LORD, which He had not commanded them. So fire went out from the LORD and devoured them, and they died before the LORD." Here were two young men brought up under the godly influence of their father Aaron, so they had no excuse for familiarity with sacred things. Nevertheless, because of self-effort they offered strange fire before the Lord, thus bringing death into the pot.

So much service today is lifeless because of self-effort! Instead of obeying the Lord's commands we go our selfish ways and offer strange fire—the symbol of self-effort. It is a serious thing to serve God in the energy of the flesh. The inevitable result is death in the pot.

C. The Sinful Intrusion of Hophni and Phinehas for the Sake of Self-Pleasing

We are told that the two sons of Eli were ". . . priests of the LORD . . ." (1 Sam. 1:3), but because of weak parental control and their own self-pleasing they became corrupt and vile; ". . . they did not know the LORD" (see 1 Sam. 2:12; 3:13). The next chapter tells us that when ". . . the Philistines fought, . . . Israel was defeated, . . . the ark of God was captured; and the two sons of Eli, Hophni and Phinehas, died" (1 Sam. 4:11).

Self-pleasing is the very opposite of living to the pleasure of God. The Bible says that ". . . even Christ did not please himself . . ." (Rom. 15:3). As a result God broke through from heaven on at least two occasions (Jesus' baptism, and the Mount of Transfiguration) to declare, ". . . This is my beloved Son, in whom I am well pleased" (Matt. 3:17, 17:5). Throughout his life he sought to do God's will, not his own (see John 4:34; Luke 22:42). When self reverses this divine principle there is death in the pot.

D. The Sinful Intrusion of Uzzah for the Sake of Self-Respect

"And . . . Uzzah put out his hand to the ark of God and took hold of it, for the oxen stumbled. Then the anger of the LORD was aroused against Uzzah, and God struck him there for his error; and he died there by the ark of God" (2 Sam. 6:6–7). Uzzah, who was probably a Levite, had taken the responsibility of bringing the ark back to Jerusalem. At any rate, he was sufficiently aware of how the ark was to be handled. Strict instructions had been given that the ark was first to be covered by the priests and then carried by the Levites by means of poles. Until it was covered the Levites were not to look at it or touch it, lest they die (see Num. 4:5–20). But when the oxen stumbled and the ark appeared to be in danger of shifting, Uzzah intruded into an area in which he was not allowed, so inviting divine displeasure and judgment.

How often we try to save the work of God, not because of his glory, but because of our self-respect. May God ever teach us that wherever self intrudes there is poison in the pot which affects our spiritual relationship with the Lord.

Illustration

When the saintly James Harvey was a young curate, he frequently talked with a wise old plowman named Clayton. One day they discussed the subject, "What is the greatest impediment to spiritual growth and happiness?" The curate said: "Surely, to renounce our sinful self." "No," said the plowman, "the greatest difficulty is to renounce our righteous self."[4]

III. Faith's Simple Solution

Elisha said, "'bring some flour.' And he put it into the pot, and said, 'Serve it to the people, that they may eat.'

And there was nothing harmful in the pot" (4:41). The way of faith is the way of full salvation, and Elisha's action typifies the truth that Christ is the remedy for every malady. Flour, in Scripture, is a beautiful type of Christ in his resurrection life and power. It is the result of the crushing and grinding of the "bread corn." How significant, then, is the procedure of putting flour into the pot of death! This pictures what Christ did for us at Calvary, when by his perfect life and death he absorbed the poison into himself and then emerged in resurrection life.

The mixture of the flour with the stew effected a divine miracle: there was no further poison in the pot. So Elisha gave orders to serve the people and they ate without ill effects. They simply believed his word in virtue of what he had done. In terms of the New Testament, this story teaches us that the only answer to the problem of sin and self is:

A. Trusting Christ to Conquer the Power of Death

Elisha said, "'bring some flour.' And he put it into the pot, and said, 'Serve it to the people, that they may eat.' And there was nothing harmful in the pot" (4:41). Because of Christ's death at Calvary we can cry, "O Death, where is your sting? O Hades, where is your victory?"; and again: "But thanks be to God, who gives us the victory through our Lord Jesus Christ" (1 Cor. 15:55, 57). How wonderful to know that ". . . through death . . . he . . . [destroyed] him who had the power of death, that is, the devil" (Heb. 2:14). Now by identification with Christ in his death and resurrection we, too, can know victory over the deadening and defiling power of Satan in our lives.

B. Trusting Christ to Cancel the Poison of Sin

". . . And there was nothing harmful [or evil, marginal rendering] in the pot" (4:41). It is one thing to know forgiveness and pardon in regard to the past; it is another to experience moment-by-moment deliverance over our corrupt natures (see Rom. 8:2 and Rom. 6:14). Now that Christ has nullified the poison of sin there is the sweetening influence and fragrance of the grace of Christ.

C. Trusting Christ to Control the Principle of Life

". . . Serve it to the people, that they may eat . . ." (4:41). The principle of life is reproduction. Just as the food became life and healing to the sons of the prophets, so the life of Christ in us becomes a ministry to others. Paul says, "always carrying about in the body the dying of the Lord Jesus, that the life of Jesus . . . may be manifested in our body. . . . So then death is working in us, but life in you" (2 Cor. 4:10–12). What a joy to communicate a ministry of resurrection power and blessing where death once reigned!

Conclusion

We have observed that God's purpose is ever to provide fullness of blessing for his people, while man's tendency is to thwart God's purpose by sinful intrusion leading to poison in the pot. Thank God, however, there is a glorious antidote in Christ crucified, risen, and reigning in our lives. Oh, that we might be so fully identified with him in simple faith that we can say, ". . . it is no longer I who live, but Christ lives in me; and the life which I now live in the flesh I live by faith in the Son of God, who loved me and gave himself for me" (Gal. 2:20).

The Secret of Energy
2 Kings 4:1–7

"... 'what do you have in the house?' And she said, 'Your maidservant has nothing in the house but a jar of oil'" (4:2).

Introduction

Here is an Old Testament story about Elisha and a poor widow which illustrates how the person and work of the Holy Spirit operates in a believer's life. It shows how God can take a Christian, who is a victim to spiritual depression, poverty, and bondage, and fill him with joy, richness, and liberty for effective service.

The story reveals that the woman had reached the place of bankruptcy. Faced with the shame and embarrassment of not being able to meet her obligations, she cast herself on the mercy of the man of God. Perhaps if she had sought his advice earlier she would have never reached this state of affairs. Is this a picture of your life? Have circumstances and unfulfilled obligations overwhelmed you like a flood?

If so, why have you not turned to the Man at God's right hand—Jesus—and asked for his guidance and intervention in your situation?

When the widow sought Elisha's advice, he asked her a most significant question: ". . . what do you have in the house? . . ." (4:2). If her reply had been, "I have nothing in the house," then Elisha would have had nothing upon which to work. The question God asks us is not so much whether we have something in the house but rather if we have *Someone* in the house of our lives.

In the passage before us, it seems reasonable to interpret the jar of oil as a symbol of the Holy Spirit in the life of the believer. Note:

I. The Identity of the Spirit in Our Lives

". . . Elisha said to her, 'What shall I do for you? Tell me, what do you have in the house?' And she said, 'Your maidservant has nothing in the house but a jar of oil'" (4:2). The New Testament teaches that there are at least two ways in which we may identify the Holy Spirit in our lives:

A. By His Indwelling

". . .'what do you have *in the house*?'. . ." (4:2). Whatever else this woman had sold or parted with, she had retained this jar of oil. Likewise whatever calamities may befall the Christian, in terms of wealth, health, or the loss of loved ones, he can never part with or lose the indwelling of the Holy Spirit. The Corinthians' church had deteriorated greatly in the absence of the apostle, having lost much of its original purity, power, and grace. Yet Paul wrote to them: ". . . do you not know that your body is the temple of the Holy Spirit who is in you? . . ." (1 Cor. 6:19; see also Rom. 8:9b, 16). So the Holy Spirit may be identified by his indwelling.

Illustration

A little girl sat at the tea table, alternately stirring and sipping her tea. Presently, with disappointment in her eyes, she exclaimed, "Mother, it won't come sweet!" The mother realized that she had forgotten to put in the sugar. This done, the sugar itself did the rest. No amount of stirring, or trying, can make our lives sweet; but when we let the Lord Jesus enter, by the power of the Spirit, he makes them pure and lovely. Sweetness of life is only possible as Jesus dwells within, exercising through us the fruit of the Spirit.

B. By His Anointing

Said the widow, ". . . Your maidservant has nothing in the house but a jar of oil" (4:2). Such a jar in the house was kept for the purpose of cooking or anointing. In normal circumstances, this oil would be used daily following the regular ablutions.

Greater than its personal use, however, was the ceremony of anointing, which was related to all the important offices of Jehovah's servants; without it he was not considered qualified for his ministry. The prophet was anointed as the messenger of God to the people (see 1 Kings 19:16). The priest was anointed that he might be holy unto the Lord (see Lev. 8:12). The king was anointed that the Spirit of the Lord might rest upon him (see 1 Sam. 16:13). Even the Lord Jesus was anointed at the outset of his ministry with the Spirit and with power (see Luke 4:18; John 3:34).

In terms of New Testament teaching, this anointing of the Spirit is distinct from the filling of the Holy Spirit, yet it is contingent upon it. It takes place initially with the new birth, but continues recurringly as the believer needs ability and authority in Christian service. Dr. C. I. Scofield said it well: "One baptism, many fillings, constant anointing." This anointing of the Spirit communicates a twofold blessing:

1. A Spiritual Ability in the Word of God

". . . the anointing which you have received from him abides in you, and you do not need that anyone teach you; but as the same anointing teaches you concerning all things, and is true, and is not a lie, and just as it has taught you, you will abide in him" (1 John 2:27). There is a distinct difference between the tuition of learning and the intuition of the Spirit. The one is intellectual knowledge; the other is spiritual knowledge. While we do not downgrade the former, we note the Bible puts the weightier emphasis on the latter. It says, ". . .'Eye has not seen, nor ear heard, nor have entered into the heart of man the things which God has prepared for those who love him.' But God has revealed them to us through his Spirit. For the Spirit searches all things, yes, the deep things of God" (1 Cor. 2:9–10). All ability in understanding the Scriptures comes through the anointing of the Spirit. Only he can open our eyes to truths that would otherwise be hidden and inexplicable.

2. A Spiritual Authority in the Word of God

"Now he who establishes us with you in Christ and has anointed us is God, who also has sealed us and given us the Spirit in our hearts . . ." (2 Cor. 1:21–22). The apostle Paul speaks of this anointing in connection with his own authority as a preacher and identifies himself with all others who are similarly anointed of the Spirit. It is an anointing of authority which carries with it a sense of God's presence and power.

Jesus promised this spiritual authority to his disciples in his final word of commission. He told them to ". . . tarry in the city of Jerusalem until [they were] endued with power from on high" (Luke 24:49). The original meaning of the word "endued" carries the thought of being invested, or clothed, with a new power. After Pentecost the disciples were to wear this power like a garment. This is why people took knowledge of these early believers, that they had been with Jesus (see Acts 4:13). This is why they were amazed and could not withstand the wisdom with which they spoke (see Acts 6:10).

Illustration

James Hervey, the friend of the Wesleys at Oxford, describes the change which took place in him through his anointing by the Spirit: that while his preaching was once like the firing of an arrow, all the speed and force thereof depending on the strength of his arm in bending the bow, now it was like firing a rifle-ball, the whole force depending on the powder back of the ball, and needing only the touch of the finger to let it off.[1]

Let me ask you, then, the question of the man of God: ". . . 'what do you have in the house?'. . ." (4:2). Can you say with deep conviction, "I have a jar of oil in the house; I know that by his indwelling and anointing the Holy Spirit indwells my life"?

II. The Reality of the Spirit in Our Lives

"And when you have come in, you shall shut the door behind you and your sons; then pour it into all those vessels, and set aside the full ones" (4:4). Whatever the pot of oil had meant to the woman in the past, she obviously had not learned the secret of its full potential and power, under God. But when Elisha took hold of the situation he indicated certain conditions in which the pot of oil would become a vital reality. There was:

A. Provided Emptiness

He commanded, ". . . Go, borrow vessels; do not gather just a few" (4:3). The value of each vessel, to this woman, was its capacity to receive. The more she provided, the more oil she obtained; when she ceased to borrow vessels the flow of oil ceased. The lesson is clear. God can only fill the capacities we make available. That is why Paul states both in Colossians and Ephesians: "Let the word of Christ dwell in you richly . . . " (Col. 3:16), while in the parallel passage in Ephesians 5:18 he commands, ". . . be filled with the Spirit." The Word of God makes the capacity in our lives; the Spirit of God fills that capacity. We have to watch, however, that our capacities are not half-filled with something else. Only as we are filled with the Holy Spirit can we expect the anointing of the Spirit.

B. Persistent Prayerfulness

". . . when you have come in," said Elisha, ". . .you shall shut the door behind you and your sons . . ." (4:4). Note that the reality and fullness of the Spirit in a believer's life is always associated with waiting on God. Luke 11:13 says, "If you, then, being evil, know how to give good gifts to your children, how much more will your heavenly Father give the Holy Spirit to those who ask Him!" Without doubt, the principle of asking applies to the initial receiving of the Spirit, as well as to the continual fullness and anointing of the Holy Spirit. Asking is praying, and the praying which counts—and *costs*—is behind shut doors. This means shutting out the many legitimate, and often pleasant, calls and demands of business, domestic, and social life.

Illustration

J. Wilbur Chapman, Presbyterian clergyman and evangelist, once met the famous missionary, "Praying Hyde," and asked him to come to his room and pray for him. Chapman had been conducting meetings at the time and very much felt the need of spiritual strengthening. Hyde graciously consented to his request, entered the room, and

locked the door. Once they were on their knees, Chapman recalls that he waited five minutes before Hyde uttered a single syllable. So special was the sense of the Lord's presence that Chapman felt hot tears beginning to course down his cheeks although Hyde had not uttered a word. Then looking heavenward, the missionary exclaimed, "O God" and again there was silence. At last, when he sensed that he was in right communion with the Lord, Hyde continued his prayer, uttering such heartfelt petitions as Chapman had never heard. Commenting later, the evangelist said, "I arose from my knees knowing what real prayer was!" Be it ours to learn that one of the great secrets of prayer is prayer in secret.[2]

C. Perpetual Yieldedness

Said the man of God, ". . . you shall . . . pour . . . into all those vessels, and set aside the full ones" (4:4). What a moment this was! How far was the woman prepared to prove the prophet's promise by submitting herself to the pouring out of the oil? Though the idea appeared fantastic, in simple faith she yielded and the miracle happened. So, too, in the spiritual life, it is only as we personally yield to the indwelling Spirit that his life begins to flow in us and from us (see Acts 5:32). The story shows us that in keeping with Elisha's word the jars of oil were filled according to the capacity provided. God will do the same for us if only we are empty, prayerful, and yielded. Only one Man in the universe possessed the Holy Spirit without measure and that was the Lord Jesus (see John 3:34).

Illustration

When General William Booth was in his eighties he was asked his secret for success. After a moment's pause for reflection, he replied, "I will tell you the secret: God has had all there was of me. There have been men with greater brains than I, men with greater opportunities; but from the day I got the poor of London on my heart, and a vision of

what Jesus Christ could do with [them], I made up my mind
that God would have all there was of William Booth. And
if there is anything of power in the Salvation Army today, it
is because God has all the adoration of my heart, all the
power of my will, and all the influence of my life." His ques-
tioner went away from that meeting knowing that "the greatness of a man's power is the measure of his surrender."[3]

III. The Sufficiency of the Spirit in Our Lives

Once the oil had been poured out Elisha said, ". . . Go,
sell the oil and pay your debt; and you and your sons live
on the rest" (4:7). These practical words teach us that the
sufficiency of the Spirit is a blessing which relates to
everyday life and also to our ministry. Note from the story
that the sufficiency of the oil provided for the following
obligations:

A. Public Accountability

". . . Go, sell the oil and pay your debt . . ." (4:7).
There are two ways in which every believer is in debt:

1. HE IS IN DEBT TO GOD

Paul tells us that ". . . we are debtors—not . . . to
live according to the flesh" (Rom. 8:12), which
implies that we are in debt to live to God from the
moment of conversion. All time lived outside the sufficiency of God's Spirit is wasted and, therefore, lost.
That is why Paul adds, ". . . if you live according to
the flesh you will die; but if by the Spirit you put to
death the deeds of the body, you will live" (Rom.
8:13).

2. HE IS IN DEBT TO MAN

The apostle realized that he owed a debt to mankind (see Romans 1:14 in terms of his prayers, his

ministry, and the gospel). God holds us responsible for fulfilling our obligations in the gospel to every person we meet. It may be by the way we speak or simply by the way we act, but we only discharge our debts by releasing something of the sufficiency of the Holy Spirit.

B. Private Responsibility

The injunction was clear: ". . . you and your sons live on the rest" (4:7). Public accountability is an obligation which every believer must fulfill, but it in no way excuses him of personal responsibility in private life. If this principle was obeyed we would not be continually hearing of Christians who behave like saints in public but live like devils in private. God holds every believer responsible for a life of tenderness, sympathy, thoughtfulness, and humility in the home. The widow had to keep her life and that of her sons healthy, strong, and useful. What a word to husbands concerning their wives; wives concerning their husbands; parents concerning their children; yes, and children concerning their parents! In Ephesians 5:18—6:9 Paul links the fullness of the Spirit with the church, the home, and business life, and in all three we are to draw our resources from God. Only then will we be individuals who are marked by the identity, reality, and sufficiency of the Spirit.

Conclusion

Do you have a jar of oil in the house of your life? If so, provide the emptiness, give yourself to prayerfulness and yieldedness, then know and show the life of usefulness in the Holy Spirit. Let your prayer be:

For this I pray, Lord for this I plead—
Thy Spirit's fullness flood my soul;
Be Thou enthroned, Lord, within my heart,
And all my yielded life control.

                                    Stephen F. Olford

10

The Secret of Victory
2 Kings 6:8–23

"Do not fear, for those who are with us are more than those who are with them" (6:16).

Introduction

The description by which Elisha is best known throughout these chapters is that of "the man of God." The life he lived, the ministry he exercised, and the authority he displayed earned him this characterization. It is not surprising, therefore, that we find the devil attacking him at every opportunity.

In the story before us, there is an outstanding example of the hatred and hostility of the enemies of God against Jehovah's servant. In point of fact, Elisha had been exposing the plans of the Syrian armies so that attempted attacks on the king of Israel had been thwarted many times. Deeply troubled, and suspecting treachery among his servants, the king of Syria called them together to discover the source of the leakage of his military secrets. The story tells us that one of his servants said, ". . . Elisha, the prophet, who is in Israel, tells the king of Israel the words that you speak in your bedroom" (6:12).

The life of a man of God always exposes the plans and plots of the enemy. His character and ministry are a rebuke to the sin and wickedness around him. For this reason he is ever a target of vicious reprisals. This story teaches us that despite Satan's devices the man of God is invulnerable because he possesses the secret of victory. Consider:

I. The Futility of Satanic Opposition

The king of Syria said, ". . . Go and see where he is, that I may send and get him . . ." (6:13). Dothan may appear to be a very perilous place in which to be found when the king of Syria is around, but when the man of God is in the center of the will of God there is nothing to fear. He is invulnerable to satanic opposition because:

A. The Motivation of the Enemy Is Always Wrong

". . . Go and see where he is, that I may send and get him . . ." (6:13). The only motivation the king of Syria had for apprehending Elisha was that the man of God was exposing his evil designs; and that is the only motivation that Satan has for seeking to apprehend us. The enemy of souls hates the holy life for it exposes the ugliness of sin and the emptiness of hypocrisy. Jesus said that the devil was ". . . a murderer from the beginning . . ." and the father of lies (John 8:44); so what else can we expect than vicious opposition from Satan?

Illustration

Nature provides us with an illustration that closely parallels the insidious tactics employed by our adversary. According to scientists, Arctic polar bears feed almost entirely on seals. To enjoy such a meal, they sometimes resort to a cunning bit of trickery. If the hole through which the seal gets his food is near the edge of the ice, the polar bear will take a deep breath and swim under water to its exact location. Remaining below the surface, he will then make a tiny scratching sound, imitating a fish. When the charmed seal hears this, he dives in for a quick supper, only to find himself suddenly entrapped in the huge, hungry embrace of his predator.

Similarly, while the man of God is prey for the enemy of souls, thank God Satan's opposition is futile because his motivation is always wrong. The Bible says, ". . . we can do nothing against the truth, but for the truth" (2 Cor. 13:8).[1]

B. The Calculation of the Enemy Is Always Wrong

"Therefore he sent horses and chariots, and a great army there, and they came by night and surrounded the city" (6:14). With all his subtlety Satan always oversteps himself and this is dramatically illustrated in this story. Since the king of Syria was aware that Elisha knew his whereabouts, it seems strange that he should try to trick the very man who knew all his secrets. Furthermore, the king of Syria had miscalculated the fact that the biggest army he could command was no match for the hosts that were supporting the man of God. How true are the words, ". . . If God is for us, who can be against us?" (Rom. 8:31); and again: ". . . He who is in you is greater than he who is in the world" (1 John 4:4).

We see then that satanic opposition is utterly futile when it is pitted against a man like Elisha. How this should comfort the godly and challenge others to seek and pursue holiness! Such a guided life is also a guarded life.

Illustration

A little boy came to his father and asked, "Father, is Satan bigger than I am?" "Yes, my boy," said the father. "Is he bigger than you, Father?" "Yes, he's bigger than your father." The boy looked surprised, but thought again and asked, "Is he bigger than Jesus?" "No, the Lord Jesus is bigger than he is." The little fellow, as he turned away, said with a smile, "Then I'm not afraid of him."

> Did we in our own strength confide,
> Our striving would be losing,
> Were not the right Man on our side,
> The Man of God's own choosing . . .[2]
>   Martin Luther

II. The Reality of Spiritual Revelation

"So [Elisha] answered, 'Do not fear, for those who are with us are more than those who are with them'" (6:16). It seems to be a principle of spiritual experience that God graciously gives special revelations to his own people under the pressure of opposition and persecution. Job was given his greatest vision of God under pressures that almost killed him. Daniel proved that Jehovah vindicates his own—even in a den of lions. Paul wrote some of his greatest epistles while chained in a Roman dungeon; and John saw the unveiling of the enthroned Christ and the eternal destinies of men and women while exiled on the isle of Patmos. This was the case with Elisha on this occasion. Encircled with satanic opposition:

A. The Man of God Saw Invisible Realities

". . . Do not fear, for those who are with us are more than those who are with them" (6:16). Like Moses before him, Elisha endured ". . . as seeing him who is invisible" (Heb. 11:27). Long before his servant knew what he was talking about, Elisha had seen beyond the Syrian army to invisible hosts of angelic guardians surrounding and protecting him. So he could say with calm composure, ". . . Do not fear, for those who are with us are more than those who are with them" (6:16). Doubtless, in his quiet time early that morning, God had given him a vision of his plan and power of deliverance.

From this we learn that when a believer is in the center of God's will Satan's attacks do not ultimately hinder, but only serve to make spiritual and eternal truths all the more precious and real.

B. The Man of God Shared Invisible Realities

"And Elisha prayed, and said, 'LORD, I pray, open his eyes that he may see.' Then the LORD opened the eyes of the young man, and he saw. And behold, the mountain was full of horses and chariots of fire all around Elisha" (6:17). Only the man who has seen spiritual visions himself can make invisible realities clear to others. It appears that while Elisha's servant was busy ministering day by day he was oblivious to the invisible realities which were being enjoyed by his master. But under the pressure of satanic attack, Elisha was able to pray effectively for his servant, so that his spiritual eyes were opened to behold the mountain full of horses and chariots of fire.

The lessons are clear. Once we have caught a glimpse of heaven our praying power assumes a new dimension, and miracles take place: people around us who are spiritually blind begin to see what we see. We also find that in Christ we are invulnerable because the greater the opposition from the enemy, the deeper becomes our spiritual experience.

Illustration

The Southern Baptist Convention was organized in 1845 in the First Baptist Church of Augusta, Georgia. As a tribute to the faith of its founding fathers, the church placed this inscription in the building: "Men who see the invisible, hear the inaudible, believe the incredible, and think the unthinkable!"[3]

III. The Authority of Sovereign Vindication

"So when the Syrians came down to him, Elisha prayed to the LORD, and said, 'Strike this people, I pray, with blindness.' And He struck them with blindness according to the word of Elisha" (6:18). A man who keeps in the center of God's will never has to justify himself; God ultimately vindicates his own. This is exemplified in this historical record of Elisha and the opposing armies of Syria. Notice carefully that the sovereign vindication of Elisha was demonstrated in a twofold fashion:

A. The Man of God Was Gloriously Delivered

In answer to prayer, God struck the Syrians ". . . with blindness according to the word of Elisha" (6:18). Could anything be more confirmative for the prophet of the Lord? God acted according to the word of Elisha. If this is not vindication, then nothing else could be. The same will be true of us, if we know what it is to be yielded to the sovereign will of God. He will always vindicate His own by a glorious deliverance—if not immediately then ultimately.

Amplification

Dr. Bob Cook, radio broadcaster, and former president of King's College (New York) once said: "You never need lift a finger to defend yourself unless you are not quite sure that God can handle the matter. Wait. Wait for time, and wait for God, and strangely enough, wait for yourself! You see, you are not in any sense static—you are constantly changing, growing, advancing, learning, moving along the road of life. If you don't have the answer to some problems in your personality, or in your relations to friends, loved ones, and relations, today—just commit it to the Lord, and wait. You'll find yourself saying, some day soon, 'Now why didn't I think of that before?'"

B. The Foes of God Were Gloriously Defeated

". . . So the bands of Syrian raiders came no more into the land of Israel" (6:23). This defeat of the Syrians is worthy of careful study. There was nothing cruel or murderous about Elisha's approach to his enemies; indeed, his whole attitude is an outworking of the teaching of the Sermon on the Mount. In his triumph over the enemy:

1. HE REDUCED THE SYRIANS TO A STATE OF HARMLESSNESS

". . . And he struck them with blindness . . ." (6:18). No purpose is served in challenging Elisha's strategy in leading the Syrian raiders into the city of Samaria. Elisha was a man of God; therefore, he would not act unethically. Some have suggested that he employed a military technique in misleading his captives while they were blinded and deluded. Another explanation is that he was quite correct in telling the Syrians that the man they sought was in Samaria—for Elisha actually lived in the city of Samaria.

The principle here is that through the victory which Christ affords us we can always render the enemy harmless. This is what Jesus did in relation to Satan, when he died on the cross. Our enemy is very much alive, but he has been rendered inoperative and harmless to the child of God who uses the right weapons of warfare—even to the pulling down of strongholds (see 2 Cor. 10:4). John tells us that the faithful ". . . overcame him [the devil] by the blood of the Lamb and by the word of their testimony . . ." (Rev. 12:11). The very word *overcame* means "to render the enemy harmless." Hallelujah for such victory!

Illustration

An Indian gentleman went to Paris, got in with the wrong crowd, became a theosophist, then a spiritist, and was much used as a medium. Eventually, he was converted to

God. Then it was that the evil spirits distressed him. For months he was awakened by them night after night, rarely getting half an hour's consecutive sleep. Tangible hands touched him, and terrible manifestations of their presence afflicted him. He prayed to God but got no relief. At last a voice appeared to say to him, "Mention the blood." He then spoke to them, commanding them by the precious blood of Jesus Christ to leave him. Every time he mentioned the blood they left him, and by that means he received complete deliverance.[4]

2. HE REDUCED THE SYRIANS TO A STATE OF HELPLESSNESS

"So it was, when they had come to Samaria, that Elisha said, 'LORD, open the eyes of these men, that they may see.' And the LORD opened their eyes . . ." (6:20). Can you imagine the panic and paralysis which overwhelmed the king of Syria and his men when they found themselves at the mercy of the king of Israel. Had Elisha given the word they would have been massacred in cold blood. But there is more than one way of overcoming evil, as we shall see from the teaching of the New Testament.

3. HE REDUCED THE SYRIANS TO A STATE OF HOPELESSNESS

". . . he prepared a great feast for them . . ." (6:23). Now while Elisha was up against flesh and blood, the forces behind these Syrians were spiritual wickednesses; yet the New Testament principle of retaliation (that of leaving all vengeance to God) applied in both instances. Note the words of the apostle Paul: "Beloved, do not avenge yourselves, but rather give place to wrath; for it is written, 'Vengeance is mine, I will repay,' says the Lord. 'Therefore if your enemy hungers, feed him; If he thirsts, give him a drink; for in so doing you will heap coals of fire on his head'" (Rom. 12:19–20). The apostle may well have had Elisha in mind when he wrote these words.

So Syria was gloriously defeated, and they ". . . came no more into the land of Israel" (6:23). While the name and the fame of the man of God spread far and wide, the Syrians feared him even more because they had discovered that he was invincible. There are many incentives to a holy life. The supreme one is that of glorifying God and enjoying him forever. But there are other motivations that drive us to know this holy walk with the Lord. One is that of being kept from the evil one. John the apostle reminds us that ". . . whosoever is born of God sinneth not, but the begotten of God keepeth him, and that wicked one toucheth him not" (see 1 John 5:18, marginal rendering). What peace and poise this brings into the Christian's life!

Conclusion

Do you know what it is to be kept from the evil one? Are you impervious to the attacks of the enemy? You can be, if you are prepared to be a man of God. Only then will you know the futility of satanic opposition, the reality of spiritual revelation, and the authority of sovereign vindication. God make us all Elishas of the twentieth century!

Part 3

Meet These Men

A Lesson in Failure: *Samson*
Judges 16:15–22

Introduction

Samson was the product of a miraculous conception and a motherly consecration. From earliest days he was to be ". . . a Nazirite to God . . ." (13:5). While he maintained his sacred vows he ". . . tore [a] lion apart as one would have torn apart a young goat . . ." (14:6), he killed one thousand men with the jawbone of a donkey (see 15:15), he carried away the gates of the city of Gaza (see 16:3), and thereby became famous as the strongest man who ever lived. In spite of his illustrious start, he never fully mastered his carnal appetites, and as a result ended his life in captivity and tragedy. The story of Samson covers four chapters in Judges (13–16); but our focus here touches on three aspects of his life.

I. The Restraining Favor in His Life

Early in his career it is recorded that ". . . the LORD blessed him" (13:24), and throughout the rest of his days this divine favor was the *only* restraining element in his life. This blessing was to be conditional on the basis that he remain ". . . a Nazirite to God . . ." (13:5). From Numbers 6:1–8 we learn that the Nazirite vow involved:

A. Separation from Worldly Stimulation

"He shall separate himself from wine and similar drink . . ." (Num. 6:3). Old Testament priests were forbidden to drink wine when they entered the tabernacle lest they die (see Lev. 10:9). Wine, in Scripture, is referred to as "a mocker" (Prov. 20:1). ". . . it bites like a serpent, and stings like a viper" (Prov. 23:32). In this context, it is a symbol of worldly stimulation and irresponsible living. This is why Paul warns the believers in Ephesus ". . . not [to] be drunk with wine, in which is dissipation . . ." (Eph. 5:18).

We live in a time when artificial attractions are designed to lead God's people astray. You only have to read the newspapers, listen to the radio, watch TV, or walk the streets of our cities to sense the pressure of the enemy. His temptations are packaged so seductively that they are almost impossible to resist.

Illustration

During the great Welsh Revival a notorious drunkard was converted. His life was changed so that all who met him knew that he was a new creature in Christ. The proprietor of the local pub was sorry to lose such a good customer, so he called out to him one day as he passed the liquor establishment, "What's gone wrong, Charlie? Why do you keep going past instead of coming in?" Charlie thought for a moment, and then replied, "Sir, it is not just that *I* keep going past; it is rather that WE keep going past—*Jesus and I.*" This Welsh convert had learned that faith unites us to the living Christ so that his life flows through us, and his Spirit indwells and empowers us.[1]

B. Separation from Worldly Reputation

"All the days of the vow of his separation no razor shall come upon his head . . ." (Num. 6:5). Long hair is a dishonor to a man (see 1 Cor. 11:14), and so was a visible sign of Nazirite separation and willingness to bear reproach for the Lord's sake. It beautifully typifies the humility and obedience of our Lord who ". . . made himself of no reputation . . ." in order to fulfill the will of his Father, even unto death (Phil. 2:7–8).

Once again, the principle has application to our day. Pressure is put on individuals to be No. 1, to parade their personalities and achievements, to attain celebrity status. Bearing reproach for the name of Christ is an unpopular doctrine in our contemporary culture. Yet the Bible is clear: ". . . do not be conformed to this world, but be transformed by the renewing of your mind, that you may prove what is that good and acceptable and perfect will of God" (Rom. 12:2).

Amplification

Andrew Murray once said: "Humility is perfect quietness of heart. It is to expect nothing, to wonder at nothing that is done to me, to feel nothing done against me. It is to be at rest when nobody praises me, and when I am blamed or despised. It is to have a blessed home in the Lord, where I can go in and shut the door, and kneel to my Father in secret, and be at peace as in a deep sea of calmness, when all around and above is trouble."[2]

C. Separation from Worldly Putrefaction

"All the days that he separates himself to the LORD he shall not go near a dead body" (Num. 6:6). The Scriptures warn: "Come out from among them and be separate. . . . *Do not touch what is unclean . . .*" (2 Cor. 6:17). Putrefaction is the "unclean" thing and we are not to touch it. This is why the Bible commands, "Do not be

unequally yoked together with unbelievers . . ." (2 Cor.
6:14) and then spells out the practical implications:

1. THERE MUST BE NO FELLOWSHIP WITH UNHOLY PRACTICES

". . . what fellowship has unrighteousness with
lawlessness? . . ." (2 Cor. 6:14). A Christian has no
business involving himself with unscriptural practices which are displeasing to the Lord—whether it
be speeding, income tax evasion, or some other uneth-
ical procedure in the home, the church, or the world.

2. THERE MUST BE NO FELLOWSHIP WITH UNHOLY PLEASURES

". . . what communion has light with darkness?"
(2 Cor. 6:14). John 3:19 tells us that ". . . men loved
darkness rather than light, because their deeds were
evil." We are to ". . . have no fellowship with the
unfruitful works of darkness . . ." (Eph. 5:11). If pleasure cannot be enjoyed in the light of God's Word and
with his approval, then it is unclean and we must
avoid it.

3. THERE MUST BE NO FELLOWSHIP WITH UNHOLY PROPHETS

". . . what accord has Christ with Belial? . . ."
(2 Cor. 6:15). While the name *Belial* refers here to
Satan, it also describes false prophets. The true
believer has no right to compromise with men who
preach and perform the work of Satan.

4. THERE MUST BE NO FELLOWSHIP WITH UNHOLY PEOPLE

". . . what part has a believer with an unbeliever?"
(2 Cor. 6:15). While we are *in* the world to try and
win the lost, we are not to be *of* the world, subscrib-
ing to their false philosophies and practices of infi-
delity. This rules out the unequal yoke in marriage,
business, or apostate affiliations.

5. THERE MUST BE NO FELLOWSHIP WITH UNHOLY PLACES

". . . what agreement has the temple of God with idols? . . ." (2 Cor. 6:16). An idol is a substitute for God, and when anything takes the place that God should have in our lives it is time to separate ourselves from it. J. Wilbur Chapman had a rule that governed his life. He said, "Anything that dims my vision of Christ, or takes away my taste for Bible study, or cramps my prayer life, or makes Christian work difficult, is wrong for me, and as a Christian I must turn away from it."

All these principles were implied in the vows that determined the favor of God in the life of Samson—and they will determine the blessing of God in our lives, too. We cannot mock the Almighty. ". . . whatever a man sows, that he will also reap" (Gal. 6:7).

Illustration

A Scotsman who greatly admired the thistle sent a few seeds to a friend living in Australia. When it arrived, the custom officers thought little of it, seeing it was only one package, and let it through, being assured it would only be sown in a private garden. Today, entire districts of Australia are covered by thistles which have become the farmer's plague. Sin, too, is like that thistle. At first it does not appear harmful; in fact, pleasurable. But left unchecked, it will spread to greater and important areas of our lives.[3]

II. The Recurring Failure in His Life

We read that ". . . Samson went *down* to Timnah . . ." (14:1). It is perilous and ominous when a Christian starts "going down." The name *Timnah* means "portion assigned," and it is quite obvious that in going down to Timnah Samson was leaving his God-given task to align himself

with the Philistines. From this point onward the recurring
failure of Samson was *compromise with the world.*

A. There Was Contamination by the World

". . . he turned aside to see the carcass of the lion . . ."
(14:8). On his journey to Timnah he encountered a lion,
and when the beast roared at him, the Spirit of God
came upon him mightily and he tore the lion apart as
if it had been merely a goat. That was good, and demonstrated the power of the Holy Spirit to overcome the
devil, who ". . . walks about like a roaring lion, seeking
whom he may devour" (1 Peter 5:8).

Samson forgot that after the greatest attestation comes
the greatest temptation. No hour is so dangerous in our
lives than after a great victory. Some time later, he
returned the same way and found the dead lion with a
swarm of bees and honey in the carcass. This is where
he compromised and violated his vows as a Nazirite.
He took the honey and shared it with his mother and
father without telling them where he had found it.
Honey is sweet, but so are ". . . the passing pleasures of
sin" (Heb. 11:25). How easy it is to rationalize sin when
honey is melting in our mouths! How we need to watch
this matter of contamination by the world!

Illustration

We all recall the sugar-coated pills our mothers used to
give us as children when we became sick. We loved those
pills at first—they were so sweet—but when we had sucked
the sugar off, they were so bitter that we wanted to spit
them out. Sin's pleasures are like that: sweet to the taste,
then the remorse and pain.[4]

B. There Was Capitulation to the World

"[Samson] told [Delilah] all his heart, and said to her,
'No razor has ever come upon my head, for I have been

a Nazirite to God from my mother's womb. If I am shaven, then my strength will leave me, and I shall become weak, and be like any other man'" (16:17). Weakened by compromise, Samson now found himself caressed in the arms of Delilah; and under seductive pressure divulged the secret of his strength. Before he knew it, ". . . the seven locks of his head . . ." (16:19) had fallen to the ground, and tragedy followed. We read that ". . . Samson . . . awoke from his sleep, and said, 'I will go out as before, . . . and shake myself free!' But he did not know that the LORD had departed from him" (16:20).

Unfortunately, this sad story is being repeated in the lives of Christians today. Flirting with the world not only paralyzes spiritual strength, it nullifies authentic witness, and is obnoxious to God (see James 4:4). When we flirt with the world we fail in the church; and this explains why a worldly church is under the condemnation of God.

Amplification

When we become a friend of the world, we take our stand in defiance of God. And, God views it as an act of an enemy, an act of espionage against Him. It is as if we were conducting guerilla warfare against the Lord. We are aiding and abetting the enemy—the same sin committed by Judas. We ask, "How could a man be so black-hearted as to betray Jesus with a kiss of brotherhood?" We are aghast at this most infamous deed in human history. But is that deed any more treacherous than for us to name the name of Jesus Christ but to serve the camp of the enemy?[5]

C. There Was Cohabitation in the World

". . . the Philistines took [Samson] and put out his eyes, and brought him down to Gaza. They bound him with bronze fetters, and he became a grinder in the prison" (16:21). Although called by God to judge Israel,

and endued with miraculous power to accomplish his
work, he ended up in captivity to his enemies. This captivity cost him his strength, his sight, and his service.
No longer was he the mighty Samson; instead, he was
just an ordinary man. No longer could he see the mighty
acts of God; instead, he was as blind as any beggar in
Gaza. Worst of all, no longer could he serve God as a
true Nazirite; instead, he ground corn in prison, as
would a woman slave—the ultimate humiliation! What
a warning this should be to you and me! This is why
the Lord Jesus asked, ". . . when the Son of Man comes,
will he really find faith on the earth?" (Luke 18:8). When
this happens Satan rejoices and the Philistines have a
heyday.

III. The Redeeming Feature in His Life

"Then Samson called to the LORD, saying, 'O Lord GOD,
remember me, I pray! Strengthen me, I pray, just this once,
O God, that I may with one blow take vengeance on the
Philistines for my two eyes!'" (16:28). How comforting to
know that there is no situation that God cannot redeem,
if there is repentance and faith on our part. The redeeming
feature in the life of Samson was that *he was a mighty
man of faith in a time of doubt and spiritual declension*
and God honored this faith (see Heb. 11:32). Like Peter,
whose faith was strengthened through failure, Samson also
emerged from defeat with one climactic feat of triumph.
Notice carefully:

A. His Restoration Through Faith in God

". . . the hair of his head began to grow again after it
had been shaven" (16:22). The evidences of his separation unto God began to reappear, and his prayer life
came alive again. He prayed, "O Lord GOD, remember
me, . . . Strengthen me . . ." (16:28), and God heard his

prayer. Praise God, there is cleansing and restoration for the penitent (see 1 John 1:9). Were it not for that glorious statement in the Word of God we would be of all men most miserable.

Illustration

In ancient history Julius Caesar had a friend to whom he gave a very generous present. When he offered it, the friend said: "This is too much for me to receive." The emperor replied, "But it is not too much for me to give." After all our sinfulness and rebellion, God's gift of pardon through Christ is almost too much for us sinners to receive; but the riches of divine mercy are not too much for him to give.[6]

B. His Vindication Through Faith in God

". . . Strengthen me, . . . that I may . . . take vengeance on the Philistines . . ." (16:28). The Philistines were gathered to sacrifice to their god Dagon and to rejoice over the capture of Samson. When they were merry with wine, they brought Samson into their midst to make sport of him. Some scholars maintain that he was made to dance and ply his riddles, as he did in his days of compromise with the world. This must have deeply grieved this man of faith. And so during a lull in the proceedings, he asked the young man who was guiding him to take him to the central pillars of the building. Then after lifting his heart in prayer to God for strength, he braced himself, and with one marvelous exhibition of strength he brought the building down upon his enemies and himself. ". . . So the dead that he killed at his death were more than he had killed in his life" (16:30).

Herein is a divine principle. Only when we die to all of self can we expect ultimate victory. For Samson, it meant physical death; for you and me, it means judicial death (see Rom. 8:13). Samson held his life cheaply in order that he might be the instrument for God's judgment. We, too, must be ready to hazard our lives if we are going to achieve the purposes of God in our generation.

Verse 31 tells us that following the collapse of the building Samson's brothers and all his father's household ". . . came down and took him, and brought him up and buried him between Zorah and Eshtael. . . ." In that quiet place Samson's mighty frame was laid to rest. Similarly, only as we die to ourselves will we know rest; for the Scriptures tell us that ". . . he who has entered his rest has . . . ceased from his works . . ." (Heb. 4:10).

Conclusion

Samson's life is both an indictment and an encouragement to those of us who are called to live by faith. We can know a restraining favor through the blessing of God, we can know a recurring failure through compromise with the world, but, supremely, we can know a redeeming feature through the triumph of faith. No wonder we are told in four different places in the Bible: ". . . the just shall live by faith" (see Hab. 2:4; Rom. 1:17; Gal. 3:11; Heb. 10:38).

12

A Lesson in Faithfulness: *Caleb*
Joshua 14:6–15; 15:13–14

Introduction

Caleb was a foreigner by birth. His father, Jephunneh the Kenizzite, was outside the circle of God's chosen people. Though disadvantaged by nativity, he went on to achieve greatly. He became possessor of "a different spirit" (see Num. 14:24) and was thereafter numbered among the people of God.

Is that the story of your life? Have you received God's spirit of adoption and become a fellow citizen with the saints and members of the household of God (see Eph. 2:19)? Unless you have, you cannot follow the deeper lessons that are to be learned from this great patriot of ancient Israel. As we briefly survey the story of Caleb, we are immediately impressed with four distinctives in his life. Observe that:

I. Caleb Knew a Surrendered Life

". . . I wholly followed the LORD my God" (14:8). Given the "new spirit," Caleb despised the halfheartedness of men who vacillate on the periphery of God's great purpose for their lives. It was either God's best or nothing at all. No wonder he earned the name *Caleb* meaning "all heart," which suggests the Hebrew idea of "dog." Just as a good dog is faithful, alert, and obedient to his master's commands and movements, so Caleb wholly followed the Lord his God. His life of surrender is referred to in a three-fold way:

A. There Was the Affirmation of His Surrender

Caleb could say, ". . . *I* wholly followed the LORD *my* God" (14:8). This was not proud boasting, but spoken with a clear conscience. A moment had come in his life when he had handed his life to the Lord with unreserved submission; following the pathway of discipleship with undeviating obedience.

We must never be satisfied with merely an intellectual awareness of how to live. God expects obedience, and there is no substitute for this.

Illustration

In his book, *Fresh Bait for Fishers of Men,* Louis Albert Banks tells an incident that illustrates what it means to be a good soldier of Jesus Christ. On one occasion while Sir Henry Brackenbury was a military attaché in Paris, he was conversing with the distinguished statesman Gambetta, who said to him, "In these days there are only two things a soldier needs to know. He must know how to march, and he must know how to shoot." The Englishman quickly responded, "I beg your pardon, but you have forgotten the most important thing of all!" "What is that?" asked the Frenchman. Brackenbury replied, "*He must know how to obey!*"[1]

B. There Was the Attestation of His Surrender

Moses, the friend of God, could say of Caleb, ". . . *you* have wholly followed the LORD my God" (14:9). Moses was ". . . learned in all the wisdom of the Egyptians, and was mighty in words and deeds" (Acts 7:22). Recent research reveals that Moses was probably the best trained man of his generation—academically, militarily, spiritually—if not of all time. For forty years he had been under the discipline of God and knew how to discern the nature of reality, so to have him confirm that Caleb wholly followed the Lord his God is important to note here. It is one thing to claim that you know a surrendered life, but quite another for others to testify to this fact.

Illustration

T. J. Bach tells in his book, *God's Challenge for Today*, of a lady who testified publicly that she had entered into a deeper relationship with God. When asked if she had experienced more power in her life or she had more important work assigned to her, she answered, "No, I don't think so. But I have noticed that my children put more confidence in me, and that my friends now frequently ask me for counsel and prayer." Says Brother Bach, "When God brings you close to himself, people will soon know about it."[2]

C. There Was the Acclamation of His Surrender

God could say, ". . . Caleb . . . has followed Me fully . . ." (Num. 14:24). What an accolade for a man to receive such a divine commendation! The fact of the matter is that Caleb was a truly surrendered man; he entertained no divided loyalties. He knew what it was to surrender his entire personality as "a living sacrifice" (Rom. 12:2).

What a challenge this brings to our contemporary age! In an hour when commitments are tentative and convictions are nebulous, how we need to reexamine the nature of true surrender to all the will of God. Only people of this caliber can impact the world outside.

Illustration

To one who asked him the secret of his service, George Mueller said: "There was a day when I died, utterly died"; and as he spoke he bent lower and lower until he almost touched the floor—"died to George Mueller, his opinions, preferences, tastes, and will—died to the world, its approval or censure—died to the approval or blame even of my brethren and friends—and since then I have studied only to show myself approved unto God."[3]

II. Caleb Knew a Spared Life

He could write: ". . . the LORD has kept me alive . . ." (14:10). While these words refer primarily to his longevity, they certainly cannot be limited to this. Caleb was a man who never stopped growing. Instead of witnessing his gradual decline, the years only served to increase his stature and enhance his prestige. The physical was more than matched by the vitality of his moral and spiritual life. In keeping him alive, God spared him from three destructive forces that afflict any man or woman who is not wholly surrendered to the Lord.

A. Caleb Was Spared from Discouragement

". . . my brethren who went up with me made the heart of the people melt, but I wholly followed the LORD my God" (14:8). While the children of Israel were discouraged, when approaching the walled cities of Canaan, Caleb and Joshua were able to take a cheerful view of the situation: all because they wholly followed the Lord. Caleb "quieted the people" (Num. 13:30)—an act of dauntless courage; he was prepared to stand alone against the tide of popular opinion.

This is one of the most crucial tests for young people who naturally crave for popularity. It is sometimes agonizing to oppose a course of action when "everyone is doing it." Men who can overcome discouragement are beyond price in our churches, offices, and homes today. It is a task that angels might worthily covet; but it is the secret of those who know wholehearted surrender to God.

William Jennings Bryan once said: "Never be afraid to stand with the minority which is right, for the minority which is right will one day be the majority; always be afraid to stand with the majority which is wrong, for the majority which is wrong will one day be the minority."

B. Caleb Was Spared from Disbelief

Concerning the rest of the children of Israel we read: ". . . they could not enter in (i.e., into the land of promise) because of unbelief" (Heb. 3:19). Here was a man whose faith laughed at impossibilities and cried "It shall be done!" His attitude was a positive one: ". . . we are well able to overcome it" (Num. 13:30). As Dr. Eadie puts it: "Caleb was brave among cowards, assured among skeptics." Nothing slays unbelief in our hearts like wholehearted surrender—that determination to go through with God, whatever the consequences.

> O for a faith that will not shrink
> Though pressed by many a foe,
> That will not tremble on the brink
> Of any earthly woe.
> William H. Bathurst

C. Caleb Was Spared from Death

"But Joshua . . . and Caleb . . . remained alive, of the men who went to spy out the land" (Num. 14:38). Moses

died. All those twenty years of age and older died, with
the exception of Joshua and Caleb. The New Testament
confirms this with these solemn words: ". . . whose
corpses fell in the wilderness" (Heb. 3:17). Paul, in his
reference to this same fact, adds: "Now all these things
happened to them as examples, and they were written
for our admonition, on whom the ends of the ages have
come" (1 Cor. 10:11).

This principle of death applies today. Paul warns:
". . . if you live according to the flesh you will die; but if
by the Spirit you put to death the deeds of the body, you
will live" (Rom. 8:13); and again: ". . . the wages of sin is
death . . ." (Rom. 6:23). In the church at Corinth many
were weak and sickly, and some had actually died
because of their disorderly walk (see 1 Cor. 11:30; 1 Peter
4:17). This may well explain strange happenings that are
taking place in religious life today. Death, for the believer,
does not mean eternal death, but does mean spiritual
barrenness and may even involve physical death.

III. Caleb Knew a Strong Life

". . . I am as strong this day as I was on the day that
Moses sent me . . ." (14:11). At 85, Caleb was strong
enough for victorious warfare. In chapter 15:14 we read
that "Caleb drove out the three sons of Anak . . ." Anak
means "giant" or "longnecked" and symbolizes the trin-
ity of evil which John describes as ". . . the lust of the flesh,
the lust of the eyes, and the pride of life . . ." (1 John 2:16).
These three forces were used by the devil to seduce Eve
in the Garden of Eden, the Lord Jesus in the wilderness,
and every true Christian here on earth.

A. There Is the Giant of Lustful Passions

". . . the lust of the flesh . . ." (1 John 2:16). The word
lust signifies a strong desire, while the "flesh" stands for

that carnal nature of fallen man which uses the body as its instrument. The flesh is thus the seat of sin in man.

Uncontrolled passions are the cause of every form of perversion in human life and are becoming a threat to our social order; in fact, it is even making tremendous incursions into church life. Caleb knew how to drive this giant out. Do you?

B. There Is the Giant of Lustful Pleasures

". . . the lust of the eyes . . ." (1 John 2:16). This is a special form of gratification. The desire may be for the artistic and aesthetic to the exclusion of fellowship with God. Pleasure has become one of our major national liabilities. Men live for the present and ignore the eternal—grasping at what they can see; they have lost all hold on what is unseen and spiritual. Here, again, the church has succumbed to the lust for pleasure. A. W. Tozer has said: "For centuries the church stood solidly against every form of worldly entertainment, recognizing it for what it was—a device for wasting time, a refuge from the disturbing voice of conscience, a scheme to divert attention from moral accountability. But of late she appears to have decided that if she cannot conquer the great god Entertainment she may as well join forces with him and make what use she can of the powers." How we need to pray, "Turn away my eyes from looking at worthless things, and revive me in Your way" (Ps. 119:37)!

C. There Is the Giant of Lustful Power

". . . the pride of life . . ." (1 John 2:16); or more literally, "the vain glory of life." Lord Acton once said, "Power tends to corrupt; absolute power tends to corrupt absolutely." Man is essentially a "show-off" because of his inherent conceit and arrogance. He will grasp at riches, seize status to become socially powerful, or he will accumulate knowledge in order to impress others. Even within religious ranks man is out for power.

Caleb was able to deal with this giant; indeed, he was more than match for all three. Though the three sons of Anak were great in size, he was greater in spirit. Though they had faces like lions they had hearts like frightened hares, and Caleb overcame them by the power of a surrendered life. Today, the believer who overcomes can only do so in the strength "which God supplies through his eternal son." ". . . For this purpose the Son of God was manifested, that he might destroy the works of the devil" (1 John 3:8).

IV. Caleb Knew a Satisfied Life

". . . Joshua blessed him, and gave Hebron to Caleb . . . as an inheritance. . . . Then the land had rest from war" (14:13, 15). Here is the ingredient of a satisfied life. God's purpose for every Christian is that he might be fulfilled. Anything less than this is frustration and defeat.

Dinsdale Young points out that "for character to be forever unrecompensed would be anomalous. It would be a blot upon the moral government of God. Either in this life or in that which is to come there must verily be a reward for the righteous . . . Caleb has had an overflowing cup in heaven throughout the ages. But he [also] had a reward whilst yet on the earth."[4] To put it simply:

A. Caleb Enjoyed the Satisfaction of Spiritual Prosperity

". . . Joshua blessed him . . ." (14:13). The sense that God is with a man, blessing his life and work, is the first ingredient in the experience of true satisfaction. When we read that ". . . Joshua blessed him . . ." (14:13) we must remember that Joshua was Israel's hero; that his name dominates the book of the triumphal entry into

Canaan—not Caleb. We are told that Israel ". . . feared [Joshua] as they had feared Moses, all the days of his life" (Josh. 4:14). So when Joshua selected Caleb from among the leaders of Israel for special approbation and anointing he was holding him up to honor as a man who wholly followed the Lord. Likewise, our heavenly Joshua wants to anoint us with the Spirit and also employ us for his glory among our contemporaries. This, in essence, is spiritual prosperity. Do you know such blessing in your life?

B. Caleb Enjoyed the Satisfaction of Spiritual Possessions

". . . Joshua blessed him, and gave Hebron to Caleb . . . as an inheritance" (14:13). This inheritance had been his by promise for 45 years; now he consciously possessed it. God has already ". . . blessed us with every spiritual blessing in the heavenly places in Christ" (Eph. 1:3), but that essential fact can only become an effectual force when we possess our possessions in Christ by an act of appropriating faith. Our heavenly Joshua has given us all things in himself and it is our privilege to enter into everything that Christ has purchased for us. Are we enjoying our spiritual possessions in Christ?

Illustration

A Texas oilman once said: "I know the man that used to own this land. He could scarcely make a living. Speculators bought up his land for a small price. They sank oil wells, and today the land is worth millions." At one time the farmer owned every drop of that oil, but he did not possess the wealth, though all of it was his. Are you enjoying your spiritual possessions in Christ?"[5]

C. Caleb Enjoyed the Satisfaction of Spiritual Peace

". . . Then the land had rest from war" (14:15). This is the final evidence of a satisfied life. This does not mean that spiritual warfare ever ceases on earth, but in answer to a full surrender the believer may know the rest of being more than conqueror. Enemies were still around Caleb, and every now and again he had to fight them, but their presence gave him no cause for worry; he was at rest in the fact that through the power of God he was victorious. Similarly, the wholly surrendered believer can overcome the strivings of the flesh by resting in the strength and power of an indwelling Christ. Caleb was satisfied because he was strong, and he was strong because he was spared, and he was spared because he was surrendered. That is what God is looking for today.

Illustration

There was once a tragic train crash. Suffering people lay trapped and dying around the scene of disaster. Presently one of the passengers recognized a gentleman who had apparently escaped unscathed. "Excuse me, Sir," asked the man, "but aren't you Dr. So and So?" "Yes," replied the doctor, "That's my name." "Well, why don't you do something?" cried the alarmed man, "Can't you see dying people all around you?" The obviously distressed doctor made this reply, "My friend, I am doing all I can, but I'm greatly handicapped: I have no instruments." Today, a bruised and dying world cries out to God, "Why don't you do something?" and back comes the reply, "I would do something, but I have no instruments." It was because Paul knew of God's need for human instruments that he pleaded: ". . . present yourselves to God, as being alive from the dead, and your members as instruments of righteousness to God" (Rom. 6:13).

Conclusion

God is still looking for human instruments that are wholly surrendered to him. Will you face the challenge and then give your answer to God?

13

A Lesson in Fulfillment: *Isaiah*

Isaiah 6:1–9

Introduction

Isaiah, whose name means "Jehovah saves," stands out as one of the greatest of the prophets. Indeed, none can so worthily be called the "evangelical prophet" as he. Through days of crisis and disaster, unprecedented in the history of his people, he constantly called his nation back to faith in the only God who could deliver.

According to Jewish tradition, Isaiah was of royal blood, or at least of noble descent. According to the Talmud, his father, Amoz, was a brother of King Amaziah, which would make Isaiah and King Uzziah cousins. His training also must have been of a high standard, for as we read his prophecy we are impressed with the majesty and originality of his thought, as well as the superlative quality of his language.

In the chapter before us we have the sensational story of his call to service and an insight into the man himself. We shall look at three aspects of his life and ministry:

I. Isaiah Was a Man Who Saw God

"In the year that King Uzziah died, I saw the Lord sitting on a throne, high and lifted up, and the train of His robe filled the temple" (6:1). News of King Uzziah's death had reached the young prophet, and in an agony of grief and sorrow he entered the courts of the temple in order that he might seek after the Lord. Up till now, an earthly throne had filled Isaiah's horizon, for the prophet was not only a member of the royal court, but had also served as a scribe to the king (see 2 Chron. 26:22).

As he waited in the divine presence, a vision broke in upon his soul—a method God often used to speak to his servants in Old Testament times. Today we have the inspired Word of God and the indwelling Spirit of God to instruct us concerning God's purposes—provided we spend time in waiting upon the Lord. The heavenly vision had to do with the glory of God, and teaches us a lesson: namely, that the holy One calls us to see him before he calls us to serve him.

A. There Was the Glory of His Person

". . . I saw the Lord . . ." (6:1). When Jesus told his disciples of Isaiah's vision he said that the prophet ". . . saw his glory and spoke of him" (John 12:41). This glory was, undoubtedly, the outshining of holiness. As Isaiah recounts this vision he tells of angelic beings known as seraphim—flaming creatures with six wings. With two they covered their faces (to indicate the attitude of holy allegiance); with two they covered their feet (to indicate the attitude of holy dependence); and with two they flew (to indicate their attitude of holy obedience). All the while they were crying to one another, saying, ". . . Holy, holy, holy is the LORD of hosts; the whole earth is full of His glory!" (6:2–3) What a lesson this must have been to the young prophet! Well does Scripture say: "Pursue . . . holiness without which no one will see the Lord" (Heb. 12:14); and we could add, ". . . without [holiness] . . . no one will [serve] the Lord."

Amplification

John Wesley said: "Bring me a worm that can comprehend a man, and then I will show you a man that can comprehend the triune God!"

Andrew Murray added: "Never try to arouse faith from within. You cannot stir up faith from the depths of your heart. Leave your heart, and look into the face of Christ."

B. There Was the Glory of His Power

". . . I saw the Lord sitting on a throne . . ." (6:1). Note that Isaiah saw the heavenly throne *in the year that King Uzziah died.* Herein is a divine principle. It is only when man is dethroned and God is enthroned that we are brought into the realization of the sovereign power of the Lord of glory. It is while God was enthroned in Uzziah's life that he reigned righteously and prosperously; but when he became self-sufficient and arrogant God had to judge him so that he died a leper (see 2 Chron. 26:23). Undoubtedly, Isaiah remembered this as he saw a filled throne in heaven. Jesus must be Lord, for "No one can serve two masters . . ." (Matt. 6:24).

Illustration

At the funeral of Louis XIV the great cathedral was packed with mourners paying final tribute to the king whom they all considered great. The room was dark, save for one lone candle which illumined the solid casket that held the mortal remains of the monarch. At the appointed time, the court preacher stood to address the assembled clergy of France. As he rose, he reached from the pulpit and snuffed

out the one candle that had been put there to symbolize
the greatness of the king. Then from the darkness came
just four words: "God only is great!"[1]

C. There Was the Glory of His Purpose

". . . Holy, holy, holy is the LORD of Hosts; The whole
earth is full of His glory!" (6:3). God's purpose is to fill
the earth with ". . . the knowledge of the LORD as the
waters cover the sea" (Isa. 11:9). If we have caught the
vision of divine service then worldwide evangelization
must be our supreme objective (see Mark 16:15; Acts
1:8). First-century Christians took this so seriously that
they reached the whole of the then-known world in some
thirty-three years. Why are we not accomplishing the
same task in our generation? Because we have lost the
vision of God. The greatest need of the church today is to
once again see the glory of God: his power and purpose.

II. Isaiah Was a Man Who Sensed God

"Then I said: 'Woe is me; for I am undone!'. . ." (6:5).
The vision of God in his holiness always creates a sense of
our own unworthiness before him (see John 16:8–11). In
the verses before us we see the outworking of this ministry of the Spirit:

A. There Was the Searching of the Spirit

Isaiah cried, ". . . 'Woe is me, for I am undone!
Because I am a man of unclean lips, and I dwell in the
midst of a people of unclean lips; for my eyes have seen
the King, the LORD of hosts'" (6:5). Six times over in the
preceding chapter Isaiah thunders out the message of
doom to his own people (see vv. 11, 18–22), but he does
not seem to sense his own need until the heavenly
vision breaks in upon him. One glimpse of the glory of

God and he is filled with a sense of guilt concerning his own sinfulness. This was so in the case of Moses, who ". . . hid his face, for he was afraid to look upon God" (Exod. 3:6); of Job, who abhorred himself and repented in dust and ashes (see Job 42:6). It was true of Peter who ". . . fell down at Jesus' knees, saying 'Depart from me, for I am a sinful man, O Lord!'" (Luke 5:8); and of Paul who, when he saw himself in the light of the heavenly vision, exclaimed: "O wretched man that I am! Who will deliver me from this body of death?" (Rom. 7:24). God has to bring us to this point before we can ever serve him; for unless we learn the nature of our own sinfulness we shall never seek the nature of God's holiness, and without holiness we cannot serve the Lord.

Illustration

Jonathan Edwards was converted through reading a single verse of the New Testament. Some hindrance had kept him from going to church one Sunday with his family. A couple of hours with nothing to do sent him listlessly into his father's library. The sight of a dull volume with no title on it evoked his curiosity, and upon opening it at random he found it to be the Bible. His eye caught this verse: "Now unto the King eternal, immortal, invisible, the only wise God, be honor and glory for ever and ever, Amen!" (1 Tim. 1:17). In his journal he writes that the immediate effect of that verse was awakening and alarming to his soul, for it brought him a most novel and extensive thought of the vastness and majesty of the true Sovereign of the universe. Out of this grew the pain of guilt for having resisted such a Monarch so long, and for having served him so poorly. Where before he had slight notions of his own wickedness, and very little poignancy of acute remorse, now he felt the deepest contrition.[2]

But the searching Spirit not only reveals the nature of our sinfulness, but also the nature of our helplessness. Isaiah exclaimed, ". . . I dwell in the midst of a people of unclean lips" (6:5). No picture more vividly portrays utter helplessness than a leper among lepers. But this is where God often has to bring his people if they would truly serve him. As long as we are self-sufficient, God can do nothing with us. This is the story of Jacob. God had to wrestle with him until his confidence in the flesh was broken. Only then could the divine Wrestler say, ". . . Your name shall no longer be called Jacob, but Israel; for you have struggled with God and with men . . ." (Gen. 32:38).

B. There Was the Sanctifying of the Spirit

"Then one of the seraphim flew to me, having in his hand a live coal which he had taken with the tongs from the altar. And he touched my mouth with it, and said: 'Behold, this has touched your lips; your iniquity is taken away, and your sin purged'" (6:6–7). In his utter sinfulness the prophet's first need was for cleansing; so the seraph took the live coal from off the altar and touched Isaiah's lips, saying, ". . . your iniquity is taken away, and your sin purged" (or atoned for, 6:7). The altar here speaks of Calvary, and the live coal suggests the application of the cross to our lives through the ministry of the Holy Spirit. Only the Spirit can bring the mortifying and purifying power of the cross to bear upon our sinful natures so that self decreases as Christ increases in all the glory of his resurrection life (see Rom 8:13). This is a process, the attitude of a lifetime where we constantly count upon the Holy Spirit to sanctify us so that we will be clean vessels, useful for the Master's work.

Illustration

A father and son were walking in a garden one spring day when the boy asked, "Father, what is gravitation?" He replied, "Gravitation, my son, is the law or principle of nature by which everything is attracted or drawn to the earth. Thus, if a stone or an apple is released, the earth draws it down, so that it falls to the ground." At that moment they passed a bed of tulips, and pointing to them the boy remarked, "Oh, but Father, look at those beautiful tulips. They all go upward; they are not drawn down." "True, my boy, but that is because in them there is another law at work! The law of life, which is stronger than the law of gravitation, has made them free from its downward pull." So, too, the Spirit of life in Christ Jesus delivers us from the penalty and bondage of sin, sanctifying us and equipping us for service.

C. There Was the Strengthening of the Spirit

"Then one of the seraphim flew to me . . ." (6:6). Just as Isaiah needed the sanctifying touch of the seraph for his sinfulness, so he required the strengthening touch of the seraph for his helplessness. This is precisely what the Holy Spirit effects in the believer's life. This is the meaning of Paul's prayer for the Ephesians when he asks that the believers might be ". . . strengthened with might through his Spirit in the inner man" (Eph. 3:16). It is out of our own sense of helplessness that we look away to God for his enabling for Christian service.

Illustration

Centuries ago a king called his most trusted herald to his side, handed him a letter, and commanded him to read it throughout the entire empire. In the letter the king offered special benefits to each subject that would improve the standard of living and promote great happiness. The only stipulation was that each person needed to appear at the nearest village square on the day the king's representative visited that village in order to collect the benefit. Similarly, it can be said that all the benefits and blessings God has for us can only be made through the Holy Spirit. He it is who enables and equips us to live the Christ-life. By his grace and his gifts we are prepared to fulfill his purpose for us.

III. Isaiah Was a Man Who Served God

". . . I heard the voice of the Lord: 'Whom shall I send, and who will go for Us?" Then I said, 'Here am I! Send me.' And he said, 'Go, and tell . . .'" (6:8–9). Purged and praising, the prophet was now ready to hear the voice of commission. This is always God's way. When we have been brought to the end of ourselves and begin a life in the Holy Spirit, we are ready to serve God responsively and receptively. Note how:

A. Isaiah Served God Responsively

His words were ". . . Here am I! Send me" (6:8). When the triune God asked the question, "Whom shall I send, and who will go for Us?" (6:8) the answer was already settled in the prophet's heart: ". . . Here am I! Send me" (6:8).

When people do not respond as readily as this it is only a painful evidence that they have never seen or sensed God in all the glory of his person, power and purpose. Are you holding back from the voice of divine appeal? Remember, the Savior travails at this very moment in his soul over a lost world. Tens of thousands die every day, and even more are born every twenty-four hours to face a world that is becoming increasingly godless, Christless, and hopeless. Have you no heart? Have you no sense of call?

Illustration

Underlying the urgent drive of Dr. A. B. Simpson was the vision he had to reach the hundreds of unreached tribes of the earth with the gospel of Jesus Christ. He said, "The sob of a thousand million of poor heathen sounds in my ear, and moves my heart: and I try to measure, as God helps me, something of their darkness, something of their blank misery, something of their despair. Oh, think of these needs! I say again, they are ocean-depths: and, beloved, in my Master's name, I want you to measure them, I want you to think earnestly about them, I want you to look at them until they appall you, until you cannot sleep, until you cannot criticize. Let their desperate plight so grip your heart, that you will pray, that you will give sacrificially, that you will say, 'Here am I, Lord, send me.'"

B. Isaiah Served God Receptively

". . . 'Go, and tell' . . ." (6:9). For the prophet Isaiah this was a commission to go and preach a message of judgment, a most unpopular and unenviable task. The commands in verse 10 to "Make the heart of this people dull, and their ears heavy, and shut their eyes . . ." involved the punitive measures which God himself would carry out. Isaiah's message would be God's instrument in doing this. The people had so persistently perverted their ways that they had gone beyond the possibility of conversion and healing.

A man may so harden himself in evil as to render his condition incurable. When here on earth, the Lord Jesus pronounced these identical words of doom on the apostate nation (see Matt. 13:14–15). Not withstanding this solemn responsibility, however, Isaiah viewed his ministry positively and redemptively. So he cried, . . . "Lord, how long will it be before they are ready to listen?" and back came the reply, "Not until their cities are destroyed—without a person left—and the whole country is an utter wasteland, and they are all taken away as slaves to other countries far away, and all the land of Israel lies deserted! Yet a tenth—a remnant—will survive; and though Israel is invaded again and again and destroyed, yet Israel will be like a tree cut down, whose stump still lives to grow again" (6:11–13, LB). How this proves that God's purpose can never be thwarted—however dark the outlook on earth! By the miracle of divine grace, the stump can grow again!

Similarly, we must not despair as we face a sinful world. The gospel is still ". . . the power of God to salvation for everyone who believes, for the Jew first and also for the Greek" (Rom. 1:16), and the word to us is ". . . 'Go, and tell' . . ." (6:9). No greater honor could be ever conferred upon men. No commission could be emphasized with greater authority. Are we prepared to go and tell? This is God's priority program until Jesus returns.

Illustration

The story is told of a heathen king who was mortally wounded in combat. As he lay dying on the battlefield he signaled to his fellow soldier to come to his side. Looking into his face he said: "Go, tell the dead I am coming." Without a moment's hesitation, that faithful servant drew his sword and plunged it into his own heart to go and tell the dead that his master was coming. That is only the tale of a heathen king; but the spirit and significance of that servant's behavior is more than challenging.

Conclusion

Jesus Christ is our King. He came once to die on a cross for our redemption. Very soon he is coming back to reign and to judge. His commission to us is to go and tell the world that he is a living Savior today, but a coming Judge tomorrow. Are we prepared to die to self, ease, and indifference to go and tell sinful men and women that Jesus saves? Only such a person has a burden and passion to win the lost at any cost.

Mine are the hands to do the work;
My feet shall run for Thee;
My lips shall sound the glorious news:
Lord, here am I; send me.

Howard W. Guinness

Endnotes

Introduction

1. Ilion T. Jones, *Principles and Practice of Preaching* (New York: Abingdon-Cokesbury, 1956), pp. 93-99.

Chapter 1

1. J. H. Bomberger, quoted in Paul Lee Tan, *Encyclopedia of 7,700 Illustrations* (Garland, Tex.: Bible Communications, 1979), p. 505.

2. J. A. Clark, quoted in Tan, *Encyclopedia of 7,700 Illustrations*, p. 1529.

3. *The Treasury of David*, vol. 4. 1950. Reprint. (London: Marshall, Morgan & Scott, 1957), p. 239.

4. *Sermons Illustrated* (Holland, Ohio, Aug. 30, 1987).

5. Ibid., April 29, 1986.

6. *The Treasury*, quoted in Tan, *Encyclopedia of 7,700 Illustrations*, p. 406.

Chapter 2

1. *Sunday School Chronicle*, quoted in Walter B. Knight, *3,000 Illustrations for Christian Service* (Grand Rapids: Eerdmans, 1952), p. 277.

2. M. R. DeHaan, *Our Daily Bread* (Grand Rapids: Radio Bible Class, April 16, 1961).

3. *Scripture Union Songs and Choruses* (Scripture Union).

Chapter 3

1. Paul Lee Tan, *Encyclopedia of 7,700 Illustrations* (Garland, Tex.: Bible Communications, 1979), p. 283.

2. *Moody Monthly*, ibid., 480–81.

Chapter 4

1. *Letters to Light-Keepers,* quoted in Walter B. Knight, *3,000 Illustrations for Christian Service* (Grand Rapids: Eerdmans, 1952), p. 300.

2. *Just a Moment,* quoted in Paul Lee Tan, *Encyclopedia of 7,700 Illustrations* (Garland, Tex.: Bible Communications, 1979), p. 1468.

3. Paul D. Robbins, "Must Men Be Friendless?" *Leadership,* vol. 5, no. 4 (Fall 1984), pp. 28–29.

4. Knight, *3,000 Illustrations for Christian Service,* p. 299.

Chapter 5

1. *Sermons Illustrated* (Holland, Ohio, Nov. 23, 1985).

2. G. Franklin Allee, ed., *Evangelistic Illustrations for Pulpit and Platform,* pp. 118–19, adapted.

3. Ibid., 137.

4. Alan Redpath, *The Making of a Man of God* (Westwood, N.J.: Fleming H. Revell, 1962).

Chapter 6

1. Walter B. Knight, *Knight's Master Book of New Illustrations* (Grand Rapids: Eerdmans, 1956), p. 267.

2. J. H. Hunter, *Saint, Seer, and Scientist,* quoted in Walter B. Knight, *Knight's Master Book of New Illustrations* (Grand Rapids: Eerdmans, 1956), p. 271.

3. *Sermons Illustrated* (Holland, Ohio, May 25, 1986).

4. Knight, *Knight's Master Book of New Illustrations,* p. 270, adapted.

5. Copyright 1935, renewed 1963 by Hope Publishing Co.

Chapter 7

1. *Christian World Pulpit,* quoted in Paul Lee Tan, *Encyclopedia of 7,700 Illustrations* (Garland, Tex.: Bible Communications, 1979), p. 529.

2. *Sermons Illustrated* (Holland, Ohio, Mar. 1, 1987).

3. *Christian Journal,* quoted in Walter B. Knight, *3,000 Illustrations for Christian Service* (Grand Rapids: Eerdmans, 1952), p. 499.

Chapter 8

1. *Sermons Illustrated* (Holland, Ohio).

2. *Choice Gleanings* (Grand Rapids: Gospel Folio Press).

3. *Christian Faith and Life,* quoted in Walter B. Knight, *3,000 Illustrations for Christian Service* (Grand Rapids: Eerdmans, 1952), p. 535.

4. Ibid.

Chapter 9

1. A. J. Gordon, quoted in Walter B. Knight, *Knight's Master Book of New Illustrations* (Grand Rapids: Eerdmans, 1956), p. 292.
2. Henry G. Bosch, *Our Daily Bread* (Grand Rapids: Radio Bible Class, Mar. 28, 1979), adapted.
3. Paul Lee Tan, *Encyclopedia of 7,700 Illustrations* (Garland, Tex.: Bible Communications, 1979), p. 1367, adapted.

Chapter 10

1. *Sermons Illustrated* (Holland, Ohio, April 15, 1986).
2. *Choice Gleanings* (Grand Rapids: Gospel Folio Press, Oct. 23, 1981).
3. Paul Lee Tan, *Encyclopedia of 7,700 Illustrations* (Garland, Tex.: Bible Communications, 1979), p. 1564.
4. *Bible League Quarterly*, quoted in Walter B. Knight, *3,000 Illustrations for Christian Service* (Grand Rapids: Eerdmans, 1952), p. 209.

Chapter 11

1. *Our Daily Bread* (Grand Rapids: Radio Bible Class, n.d.).
2. Paul Lee Tan, *Encyclopedia of 7,700 Illustrations* (Garland, Tex.: Bible Communications, 1979), p. 570.
3. *Our Daily Bread* (Grand Rapids: Radio Bible Class, n.d.).
4. A. Naismith, *1,200 Notes, Quotes, and Anecdotes* (Hammersmith: Pickering & Inglis, 1963), p. 151.
5. B. J. Chitwood, *A Faith that Works* (Nashville: Broadman Press, 1969).
6. *Our Daily Bread* (Grand Rapids: Radio Bible Class, n.d.).

Chapter 12

1. *Our Daily Bread* (Grand Rapids: Radio Bible Class, n.d.).
2. *Our Daily Bread*, quoted in Paul Lee Tan, *Encyclopedia of 7,700 Illustrations* (Garland, Tex.: Bible Communications, 1979), p. 1371.
3. *British Weekly*, ibid., 1367.
4. Dinsdale Young, *Neglected People of the Bible* (London: Hodder and Stoughton, 1901), p. 72.
5. Harold P. Barker, *Windows in Words* (Hammersmith: Pickering & Inglis), p. 116.

Chapter 13

1. Homer J. R. Elford, quoted in Paul Lee Tan, *Encyclopedia of 7,700 Illustrations* (Garland, Tex.: Bible Communications, 1979), p. 506.
2. C. H. Robinson, ibid., 501, adapted.

For Further Reading

Chapters 1–6

Barber, Cyril J., and John Daniel Carter. *Always a Winner: A Commentary for Laymen/1 Samuel.* Glendale, Calif.: Regal Books, 1977.

Blaikie, William G. *David, King of Israel: The Divine Plan and Lessons of His Life.* Minneapolis: Klock and Klock Christian Publishers, 1981.

_____. *The First Book of Samuel.* Minneapolis: Klock and Klock Christian Publishers, 1978.

Briscoe, D. Stuart. *A Heart for God.* Nashville: Thomas Nelson Publishers, 1984.

Crockett, William D. *A Harmony of the Books of Samuel, Kings, and Chronicles: The Books of the Kings of Judah and Israel.* 1897. Reprint. Grand Rapids: Zondervan, 1961–1966.

Keller, W. Philip. *David: The Time of Saul's Tyranny.* Waco, Tex.: Word, Inc., 1985.

Krummacher, Frederick W. *David: The King of Israel.* Trans. M. G. Easton. Edinburgh: T. and T. Clark, n.d.

Maclaren, Alexander. *The Life of David as Reflected in His Psalms.* New York: Macmillan, 1885.

Meyer, F. B. *David: Shepherd, Psalmist, King.* London: Marshall, Morgan & Scott, 1953.

Pink, Arthur W. *The Life of David.* 2 vols. Grand Rapids: Zondervan Publishing House, 1958.

Redpath, Alan. *The Making of a Man of God: Studies in the Life of David.* Westwood, N.J.: Fleming H. Revell Co., 1962.

Taylor, William M. *David: King of Israel.* Grand Rapids: Baker Book House, 1961.

Whyte, Alexander. *Bible Characters.* Edinburgh: Oliphants, Ltd., n.d. 2:103.

Chapters 7–10

Crocket, William D. *A Harmony of the Books of Samuel, Kings, and Chronicles: The Books of the Kings of Judah and Israel.* 1897. Reprint. Grand Rapids: Baker Book House, 1951.
Edersheim, Alfred. *Practical Truths from Elisha.* Grand Rapids: Kregel Publications, 1982.
Farrar, F. W. *The Second Book of Kings.* Minneapolis: Klock and Klock Christian Publishers, 1981.
Kirk, Thomas, and George Rawlinson. *Studies in the Book of Kings.* 2 vols. in 1. Minneapolis: Klock and Klock Christian Publishers, 1983.
Klein, Ralph W. *Word Biblical Commentary.* Vol. 10. Waco, Tex.: Word Inc., 1983.
Krummacher, Frederick W. *Elisha: A Prophet for Our Times.* Trans. R. F. Walter. Grand Rapids: Baker Book House, 1976.
_____. *The Last Days of Elisha.* Grand Rapids: Baker Book House, 1981.
Mawson, J. T. *Delivering Grace, as Illustrated in the Words and Ways of the Prophet Elisha.* London: Pickering & Inglis, 1932.
Patterson, R. D., and Hermann J. Austel. *The Expositor's Bible Commentary.* Vol. 4 (1 and 2 Kings). Grand Rapids: Zondervan Publishing House, 1979.
Whyte, Alexander. *Bible Characters.* Edinburgh: Oliphants, Ltd., n.d. 3:101.

Chapter 11

Armerding, Carl E. *Word Biblical Commentary* (Judges). Vol. 8. Waco, Tex.: Word, Inc., 1985.
Burney, Charles Fox. *Notes on the Hebrew Tests of Judges and Kings.* 2 vols. New York: Ktav Publishing House, 1966.
Bush, George. *Joshua and Judges.* Minneapolis: Klock and Klock Christian Publishers, 1981.
Cundall, Arthur E. *Tyndale Old Testament Commentary* (Judges). Downers Grove, Ill.: InterVarsity Press, 1974–.
Fausset, Andrew Robert. *A Critical and Expository Commentary on the Book of Judges.* Minneapolis: Klock and Klock Publishing Co, 1977.
Kirk, Thomas. *Samson: His Life and Word.* Edinburgh: Andrew Elliot, 1891.
Lang, John Marshall, and Thomas Kirk. *Studies in the Book of Judges.* 2 vols. in 1. Minneapolis: Klock and Klock Christian Publishers, 1983.
Whyte, Alexander. *Bible Characters.* Edinburgh: Oliphants, Ltd., n.d. 2:33.
Wood, Leon J. *Distressing Days of the Judges.* Grand Rapids: Zondervan Publishing House, 1975.

Chapter 12

Blaikie, William G. *The Book of Joshua.* Minneapolis: Klock and Klock Christian Publishers, 1978.
Bush, George. *Joshua and Judges.* Minneapolis: Klock and Klock Christian Publishers, 1981.

Ironside, H. A. *Addresses on the Book of Joshua.* New York: Loizeaux Brothers, Inc., 1950.

Meyer. F. B. *Joshua and the Land of Promise.* New York: Fleming H. Revell Co., 1893.

Pink, Arthur W. *Gleanings in Joshua.* Chicago: Moody Press, 1964.

Redpath, Alan. *Victorious Christian Living: Studies in the Book of Joshua.* Westwood, N. J.: Fleming H. Revell Co., 1955.

Scroggie, W. Graham. *The Land and Life of Rest: The Book of Joshua in the Light of the New Testament.* London: Pickering & Inglis, 1950.

Chapter 13

Alexander, Joseph A. *Commentary on the Prophecies of Isaiah.* Grand Rapids: Zondervan Publishing House, 1962.

Allis, O. T. *The Unity of Isaiah.* Philadelphia: Presbyterian and Reformed Publishing Co., 1950.

Delitzsch, Franz. *Commentary on Isaiah.* 2 vols. Reprint. Grand Rapids: Wm. B. Eerdmans Publishing Co., 1949.

Ironside, H. A. *Expository Notes on the Prophet Isaiah.* Neptune, N.J.: Loizeaux Brothers, Inc.

Jennings, F. C. *Studies in Isaiah.* Neptune, N.J.: Loizeaux Brothers, Inc., 1966.

Vine, W. E. *Isaiah: Prophecies, Promises, Warning.* London: Oliphants, Ltd., 1953.

Whyte, Alexander. *Bible Characters.* Edinburgh: Oliphants, Ltd., 3:139.

Young, Edward J. *The Book of Isaiah: The English Text, with Introduction, Exposition, and Notes.* 3 vols. Grand Rapids: Wm. B. Eerdmans Publishing Co., 1965.